THE BEST
OF THE BEST
CANADIAN POETRY
IN ENGLISH

the Best of

THE Best Canadian Poetry

IN ENGLISH

TENTH ANNIVERSARY EDITION

MOLLY PEACOCK
AND
ANITA LAHEY
SERIES EDITORS

TIGHTROPE BOOKS

Tightrope Books
#207-2 College Street,
Toronto Ontario, Canada M5G 1K3
tightropebooks.com
bookinfo@tightropebooks.com

SERIES EDITOR: Molly Peacock

ASSISTANT SERIES EDITOR: Anita Lahey

MANAGING EDITOR: Heather Wood

COPY EDITORS: Kathleen Anderson, Luka Pajkovic

COVER DESIGN: David Jang

INTERIOR DESIGN: David Jang based on an original design by Dawn Kresan

Produced with the assistance of the Canada Council for the Arts and the Ontario Arts Council.

A cataloguing record for this publication is available from Library and Archives Canada.

CONTENTS

MOLLY PEACOCK

The Best Canadian Poem Now: A Lyric Meditation Leads to Awe

The ninety poems in *The Best of the Best Canadian Poetry, Tenth Anniversary* reach from the cranium of our national thoughts down through the neck of our moral frustrations into the hearts and lungs of our personal concerns, and even to our cultural gag reflexes—just as if poetry were Canada's *vagus* nerve. The *vagus* extends nearly the length of the human body, transferring information from the heart to the brain, and importantly bringing it back again. It works in two directions, the way that the first poem of this alphabetically-arranged book, Margaret Avison's "Two Whoms, or I'm in Two Minds," describes two ways of thinking. *Vagus* shares a Latin root with *vagabond*, and *wander*, and like that nerve, both wandering and wondering drive the contemporary Canadian poem. Just as the vagus meanders, controlling heart rate, blood pressure, digestion, inflammation, immunity—even sweating—the poems here sing, meditate, mock, despair, thrill, and tease. They venture from the intense repercussions of the dynamics of the family to terrorism, from the coming extinction of species to the restorative hope of moral action.

Buried in the middle of Avison's poem is a short, rich description of the rhythmical pondering born of wondering aloud. Her meditative lyric, one of the last she wrote (at about the same time as we began our *Best Canadian Poetry in English* series), forecasts the 21st-century explosion of poetry in Canada that we celebrate here. In her fifth stanza Avison writes in the voice of her first mind, so to speak, her first "Whom": "Now permit me to insist on / elaborating the thoughts I was / headed for…," but in the next stanza the other of the poet's two minds responds,

> You plan to do
> that in
> words?

Avison epitomizes the endeavor of the poet to elaborate thoughts while second-thinking those thoughts, even as the poet is writing them! The notion of two-minds-inside-one-consciousness seems to operate across the aesthetic landscape of Canadian poetry, from conservative to experimental styles, from locales in Newfoundland to British Columbia, from world-centred viewpoints to heartland-centred standpoints, in forms sometimes short, often long, sometimes dense and abstract, sometimes clear and song-like. The two minds, one "elaborating thoughts," the other questioning and quizzical, pulse and play throughout the ninety poems we've culled. From a ten-year-old boy's warmth of observation as he watches a neighbor skinning a bear on his back porch, the animal's eyes staring "bigger and bigger until they become moons" (in Armand Garnet Ruffo's free-verse poem "The Tap is Dripping Memory") to a chilling very grown-up litany of techniques of tagging the ears and numbering the lips of bears for observation (in Samuel Garrigó Meza's prose poem "Capture Recapture") two minds, the witness and the actor, the self and the counterpoint of another, serve to create twin approaches to single events. A girl views her stepfather in Susan Elmslie's poem "Box," just as the stepfather views the girl, the poet opening these two consciousnesses through the fraught, apparently ordinary noun of the title. In "Turing's Machine" John Barton speaks in the voice of the code breaker Alan Turing, who is both an "I" and a "we," someone who is forced to lie, and who lies down, the voices of both a man persecuted for his homosexuality and that of a computer. This complex dialogue is written in the repetitive form of a pantoum. Historical speech reverberates against a contemporary sensibility in Joy Russell's poem in tercets, "On King George's Crowning," where a Jamaican voice re-interprets "the Queen's English," past events and contemporary responses perceived, felt and examined side-by-side.

When Emily Dickinson famously described poetry to her literary correspondent Thomas Wentworth Higginson in physical terms, she wrote in 1870: "If I read a book and it makes my whole body so cold no fire can warm me I know *that* is poetry. If I feel physically as if the top of my head were taken off, I know that is poetry." The vagus nerve, some researchers tell us, produces exactly that sensation: awe. Awe is that combination of thrill and fear at the vastness of experience that makes a poem transcendent. Awe conjures up both amazement and horror, anxiety, and humbleness in the face of immensity. Several decades before, in 1836, another nineteenth-century figure, Ralph Waldo Emerson, described awe in his essay "Nature," also in relation to his head: "Standing on the bare ground, my head bathed by the blithe air and uplifted into infinite space, all mean egotism vanishes. I become a transparent eyeball; I am nothing." A sense of the ego vanishing, a merging with the world, throbs at the centre of this sort of amazement. In poetry, the feeling of merging with the world thrums inside lyric meditation—a sensation that carries thinking into song, and rhythm back into thought. The ninety poets here, using microscopes and cell phones in locations from steeltowns to IKEA and in time periods from the imagined nineteenthth-century to a fantasy future in which unicorns are hunted create a kind of Canadian sublime, that is, a lyric meditation that leads to awe. Vastness of expanse—in space and in time and in moral compass—underpins even our shortest poem, Shelley Leedahl's, "Single Pansy Among Stones," where a flower tries "so hard to be the sun it hurts." The ordeal of tackling the overwhelming emerges in Laurie D. Graham's "Say Here, Here," as the poet challenges national pride, and in Steven Heighton's "Some Other Just Ones," in which the poet is determined to collect examples of generosity and authenticity—but without a shred of sentimentality.

How do these poets do it, keep on approaching the vastness of big questions, yet anchoring grandeur in the everyday? By being in two minds, of course, and keeping awe as an ultimate, subliminal subject. They tune to the basic subjects of poetry—love and death—by tapping distinct rhythms that vibrate with the life we live now. For Kayla Czaga, who tries to define what love is in "That Great Burgundy-Upholstered Beacon of Dependability," the question comes down to serious wordplay: the difference between "nightstand" and "one-night stand." For Sadiqa de Meijer, an article of clothing, a "pink salwar kameez," becomes all the varieties of existence reflected "in a hundred miniscule mirrors / compound eye of classmates, strangers, satellites / and drones… cratering / my countries." For Sue Goyette, both love and death reverberate in the prospect of her children losing their father. Multiple perceptions un-anchor the children and their mother as they assimilate the facts of this loss, yet veer off those facts, where suddenly the strawberries and tea in a funeral home become as much a thing to contemplate as their father himself.

Like the intrepid adventurers in children's stories, Canadian poets make a universe unto themselves, with parents distant. Unlike American poets, descendants of inspiringly oddball parents Whitman and Dickinson; or British poets, whose huge family tree branches from the poets of the English Renaissance; or Irish poets, basking in the mottled light and darkness of W.B. Yeats, Canadian poets who write in English are a quirky family of semi-siblings who understand their forebears more individually. Though there are distinctive, important great aunts and uncles, from Gwendolyn MacEwen to Al Purdy, a Canadian poet writing in English can happily come to the page or screen with a deep sense of the structures of poetry, often from a familiarity with verse in other languages from French to Urdu to Haida, but without an onus of obligation—simply with a thinking process.

This musing includes the full range of types of poetry, from received forms like sonnets to free-verse poems dependent on cleverly astute line breaks, to graphic poems. There is more than a bit of the essayist's impulse in a Canadian poem, even in our most abstract ones, and even in our shortest. These works of the past ten years have no trouble leaping stanzas, for unlike prose essays, they rely on the line, and they can enjamb those thoughts as Avison does: "You plan to do / that in / words?"

The unruffled pacing displays a freedom to think (and re-think) as the poet proceeds. Shirley Bear's poem "Flight," full of water imagery and waterfowl, is a stately—almost leisurely—elegy for a beloved. The poet has "walked with you forever / in the valleys of time and space." This divagation comfortably holds disparate pensées. It is simply made for the ambiguity of being of two minds. Yet even though the process of wandering can make the poem seem like it has no goal, it isn't aimless; in fact, the long pulse of the Canadian poem can issue vigorous electricity. When I first read Sandra Lambert's "Our Lady of Rue Ste Marie," I couldn't believe the litany would sustain for so many pages. That unique combination of repetition and ramble is particularly Canadian—language both ample and driven. Litanies are favored by our poets from the decade, like the tumbling, alliterative language in Kirya Marchand's "Hamlet."

Overwhelmingly, poets of the *Best of the Best* write about animals. When an animal steps onto the stage of a poem, inevitably the true self—not the social self, or the economic or family self, but the unfettered, unstructured identity of a core being—steps forward. One poet we don't claim enough, Elizabeth Bishop, famously wrote "The Moose" about a great, smelly barge of female mammal identity, topped with a modest rack of antlers that proceeds into the road, stopping a bus heading though the Maritime provinces at night. The blunt magnificence of the moose also becomes the magnificence of the poet-creator with all her shaggy faults. In this same way, the voice of Michael Crummey becomes a Minke whale viewed over and over again in slow motion; Stephanie Bolster's persona becomes the worm in her garden; Lorna Crozier's father materializes as the exotic pet bird in her poem "Seeing My Father in the Neighbours' Cockatoo." The habits of animals, whether they be insects like Mary Dalton's ant in "A Little Tin Pail," or the literary starlings in Medrie Purdham's "How the Starling Came to America: a Glosa for P.K. Page," lead readers through a process of human transformation—and to the pops of surprise that we come to poetry for.

Awe is both surprise and trepidation, sometimes dread of imperfect moral choices as it is for Julie Bruck in "Two Fish," where neglected goldfish become an emblem of human nature both damaged and thriving. In the context of animals, ideas of damage and thriving inevitably lead to questions of environmental degradation. In her crown of sonnets "A Citizen Scientist's Life Cycle," Brenda Schmidt minutely examines the flora and fauna in a culvert with extreme awareness of the wildlife around her and a weird prey-prayer. "Life is a passage and here I am, prey / preying on fear." In his poem "Little Animals," Bruce Taylor tracks the history of microbes from "the first Microscopist" through water, "the restless stuff / that sustains and dissolves us." Even Peter Chiykowski's love poem "Notes from the Canary Islands" is written from a research station, the poet trying to shout *I love you* through a satellite phone; the image of the lovers communicating is a turtle "choke-chained by telephone wires." Those lovers are our contemporary Pyramus and Thisbe, and the chink in the wall they speak through is the hope of love through a wasted environment.

Nature invests, invigorates and invades Canadian poetry, and Canadian poets over the last decade have become the voice of our nation's environmentalists. There is no innocence in the voices speaking about Canadian wilderness. They have picked up the tone of national bewilderment and grief over a landscape permanently altered, sensing it and saying it rhythmically, as Dennis Lee does in "Slipaway." If there is a leading eco-poetry in the English-speaking world, I would claim it is ours, because our poems exhibit a complexity of tone with deep description rather than judgment. These notes of mournfulness also compose dirges for the vocations that used to make a living from our land. Karen Solie's "Tractor" lies rusted in its field; Dani Couture's thousand-footer Great Lake Ship is pulled "down by torch and hand;" and Dave Margoshes' "The Chicken Coop" that never "gets rid of the stink / of chickens" is turned into a substitute house for the family homestead that was lost. Anguish over the passing of a way of life provokes questions about how we live now, about how a person should be.

In Shane Neilson's "My Daughter Imitates A.Y. Jackson's 'Road to Baie St. Paul'," a father observes his daughter imitating an iconic Group of Seven painting, wondering "Who could it be, and where is this, and why?" Neilson, a physician-poet who doggedly seeks answers, won't leave that question hanging. Both the painting and the little girl have twin answers—or perhaps twice the answer to whom, where, and why. In Lucas Crawford's "Failed Séances for Rita MacNeil (1944-2013)" and Ben Ladouceur's "I Am In Love With Your Brother," the ceremony of identity becomes the structure of poetry. Canadian poems today have a mental freedom—they follow the poet's thoughts—and the forms of the poems evolve from those thoughts, even as they might partake from elements of traditional forms in English or in other languages. Who a person is, or, in the terms of the title of a novel by Sheila Heti, *How Should a Person Be?* pulses, *vagus*-like, between the brain and the heart of our poetry of the decade.

Twenty-five years ago, when I emigrated from the United States to Canada, I would walk into a bookstore—there were many bookstores, then—and speed to the poetry section. Few of the names were familiar to me. I had searched the world for poems to represent the whirling cultural mass of New Yorkers when I co-originated Poetry in Motion on the New York City subways and buses. Even as I scoured for Greek, Japanese, Polish, Nigerian, Chilean verse, it only slowly occurred to me to search for a Canadian poem to put on a New York placard. Who were these poets, and why didn't I, an international traveler who read poetry from many countries, know about them?

My curiosity led me to an alliance with the founder of Tightrope Books, Halli Villegas. Just as she was forming the press, my idea of bringing the American tradition of choosing the best group of poems published in literary journals each year north of the border was born. Heather Wood has been with us as managing editor for this decade, and as the poets in the anthologies know, it is Heather who really is the goddess in our details. We have continued under current Tightrope publisher Jim Nason's wise guidance. *The Best of the Best* poems are almost like live creatures to me at this point. First they were survivors rescued from the avalanche of submissions by an editor of one of Canada's more than fifty print and online literary magazines. Then they weathered a sifting by one of the prominent guest editors for a long list for one of our yearly Best Canadian volumes. After that they were harrowed in the final yearly selection by the series editors—for six years that was me alone, and for the past three I was joined by the able and inspiring Anita Lahey. Together we've enthused, harangued, and sympathized with each guest editor as we've shaped each year's final fifty. Now comes the test of the decade. Our best of the best ninety have been scrutinized, sieved, and sorted—we've even provided an index by subject and form. We hope teachers, librarians, poets, students of poetry, and those generally curious about this lyric art will use our anthology. These are poems both to teach and to share.

Is it extreme to have taken on a task to read hundreds of poems per year season in and season out for the last ten years? Of course it is. Poets are extreme. Poetry itself is extreme. *Extreme* might be the single word to capture living in the early twenty-first century. Trying to educate myself, asking what is a Canadian poem, has led me to consider the enormity of how to be in the world today. And through my reading—guided by nine extraordinary guest editors—I've stumbled on a definition of a contemporary Canadian poem: *a lyric meditation that leads to awe.* Born of the electricity of thinking and reversing thoughts without fear, yet also born of the dread and wonder of contemporary existence, our current poetry represents a tattered, ragged, brilliant idea of the sublime.

"Frog jumps in pond," the classical, seventeenth-century Japanese poet Basho famously calligraphed, concluding his notoriously impossible-to-translate haiku, "then, water sound." How does the sound of a frog making a plop in a pond address the issue of Syrian immigrants or those among us now unemployable because of technological shifts? In every situation of extremis, when a human being has no control at all, poetry rises, suddenly becoming valued again. I think it surfaces as a method of control. There are two kinds of control a poem offers. First, the making of a poem gives a poet the power of arrangement. But listening to a poem gives the audience a kind of control, too.

An image with its cadence becomes something to cling to. That experience of holding on to something in the poem is, paradoxically, like being embraced. The poem seems to hold the listener in return. That, too, is a form of awe, the sublime dialog of being in two minds that winds from the Canadian cultural cranium to the Canadian civil heart.

Molly Peacock
Toronto, ON

ANITA LAHEY

Poem Seeks Temporary Home in Magazine
(Roomies Welcome; Sympathetic Editors Only, Please)

The act of poem-making requires going inward. But its deeper impulse is an opening outward, a desire to connect through this refined communiqué. So what happens when a poet emerges from that interior space, blinks, and pronounces the poem ready to speak? It's all grown up, ready to inhabit the world on its own.

The poet pours over favourite publications: might the poem find welcome here? There? Eventually, the thumb slides the cursor over "submit." The hand drops the envelope through the slot. The work's in someone else's hands now. The poet can walk away, pursue a new impulse.

Here we are, a full decade into the project of *Best Canadian Poetry in English*, which every year is a product of those brave, definitive acts: poets separating themselves from their creations. BCP series editor Molly Peacock and I (her enthusiastic "second" since 2014), took months to review the previous nine editions of the anthology, painstakingly weighing our selections for the grouping gathered here: 90 poems that wield the power they contained when first selected by a guest editor; 90 poems that continue to give, challenge and surprise; 90 poems long and short, registering a teeming marketplace of voices, techniques, passions, and concerns. Whether as far back as 2007, or as recently as 2015, each of these poems first found public audience in the readership of a literary magazine. Each was forced to contend with the judgment of the editors of that magazine, without any sympathetic intermediary, no explanation or defense, nothing and no one to speak on its behalf but the words from which it was made.

My poetry editing "career" began around the turn of the millennium. A contract writer with the National Gallery of Canada, I would inhabit an office high above the Ottawa River a few afternoons a week. My editor there was John Barton, also then co-editor of *Arc Poetry Magazine*. One day he stopped by my desk and passed me a folder. "Let me know what you think of this? There's no rush."

Inside lay a chart with names, comments, and several Ys, ?s and Ns. Beneath it, poems. This was a submission to *Arc*, and John was asking me to read it. Assess it. Me. As a journalist I'd edited articles by my peers, but the bar for acceptable journalistic work is not ambiguous. Poetry was so idiosyncratic, who was I to say what was good? Publishable? Flash to Alice Munro: *Who Do You Think You Are?* I delved in. Later, in his office, the window revealing a bright snowscape and the icebound river beyond, John encouraged me to articulate my response. The poems were puzzling, but compelling. I liked them. But the readers' comments were lukewarm. John said, "Sometimes people read too quickly." A hazard of reading submissions in high volumes.

After that, when duties at the Gallery allowed, John and I often discussed poetry submissions. Now I see these interludes as an apprenticeship: how to trust my reader's eye; how to slow down, really see a poem. John invited me to join *Arc*'s board, and when he moved west to take up the editorship of *The Malahat Review* (a position he still holds), fellow board member Matthew Holmes and I took the helm at *Arc*, which wasn't the "Ark" but nonetheless *felt* like a ship—a cumbersome container ship; a proud tall ship; a research vessel; a haven, à la Noah, for catastrophic times, which we rebuilt from the ground up issue by issue, carefully fitting together poems and hearty discussions of craft.

I toiled at *Arc* for eight years, then stepped back. But that moment when, curious, I put my work aside, and beheld that little pack of poems—I'm still in it. Still daunted, forever humbled. Ready for the thrill of encountering a poem fresh from the poet's homegrown factory, out in the world for the first time, sent on its way by its maker, with one intent: to seek readers. The poem's execution of that intent is at least in part dependent upon me and my fellow editors. The poem may be worthy of a readership, but for it to find one, we must first be worthy of the poem.

In preparation for this essay, I interviewed poetry editors from several Canadian journals. I wanted some sense, beyond my own experiences, of the poem's journey from author to submissions heap to magazine to reader to the boxes upon boxes of publications delivered to BCP guest editors each year, to this 10th anniversary anthology you're holding. My research could not be exhaustive. Consider this a collection of telling snapshots: of ready editors and bundled poems, meeting up in a variety of situations, encircled in an atmosphere of anticipation and uncertainty—both editor and poem awaiting the spark of connection.

Meet Barbara Schott, longtime poetry editor at Winnipeg's *Prairie Fire*, who routinely reviews 1,000 submissions per year. She calls this "poetry by the pound." Schott also calls regular submitters "frequent flyers." A conversation with a poetry editor can be like wading through a flow of spontaneous metaphor. Before she retired from her job as a textiles importer, Schott was a frequent flyer herself. She'd bring poetry packs on business trips from Winnipeg to Toronto or Montreal, and do her reading in the sky: "The plane time was suspended animation." Now she reads before bed, or at the lake, limiting herself to 3 or 4 submissions per sitting. "I get numb from poetry because it's so intense," she says. "And I know what it means to write and send your stuff out in the world. I'm holding somebody's very important life work in my hands." What does she hope for, as her gaze alights the page? "You're looking for language that goes beyond just description. A quality that transcends what the poem is about. It detonates something in you as a reader."

Meet Ian LeTourneau, one of three poetry editors at *The Fiddlehead* (he also manages design and layout) in the magazine's office in a 1950s Fredericton ranch house on the University of New Brunswick's hilltop campus, looking up from a half-read submission through a window with a view of the driveway—a window that, by midwinter, has been buried in plowed snow. Picture LeTourneau with longtime editor Ross Leckie (*The Fiddlehead*'s heart and soul), and their fellow editors, hashing over submissions at Reads, a café next door to Fredericton's Westminster Books. The author of a poem under consideration works in the bookshop. The editors like her poem, but have a minor revision in mind. Leckie walks next door, and returns a few minutes later, beaming. "OK, we got it!" What does Letourneau love about his job? "I think every really good poem teaches me a new way to read a poem or write a poem. It's like an infinite pool of ideas and ways of putting words together. That seems inexhaustible, which is really alluring."

Meet Barbara Carter, poetry editor at *The New Quarterly* in Waterloo, laying out snacks in her home for an evening meeting of the poetry board, whose members range from recent grad students to a bookstore owner to poets to current and retired teachers. Once gathered, they'll read aloud the top contenders from an original batch of 300 poems, which circulated among them in packs of 30 (10 poets at 3 poems each). Any poem marked "yes" or with a strong "maybe" by even a single board member has a chance. "We take a look at why it's spoken to an individual, why it appeals," says Carter. "That can range from craft to voice to originality. We all love selection meetings. There's some very friendly rivalry. The conversations help sharpen all our critical skills." A former high school English teacher, Carter came to poetry editing unexpectedly. Now, she'll fall for certain poets and read obsessively through all their books. "Poetry has become my first love. I find it immensely satisfying. It keeps my senses alive. It keeps me thinking and aware. It sharpens my way of looking at the difficult things that are happening in the world right now."

Meet *Arc Poetry Magazine*'s poetry editor Rhonda Douglas, reading submissions through *Arc*'s online portal in a hotel or café with wifi—somewhere in India, South Africa, Senegal, London, Hong Kong—grateful for the task. "The work I do is in international development," says Douglas.

"When I'm working I can be experiencing some hard things. And I'm someone who believes that poetry saves. I routinely have that experience, where at a minimal level my spirits are lifted. I have this sense of solidarity with other people for whom language is important. It's a way of understanding what it means to be human."

Meet Catriona Wright, poetry editor for the online quarterly *The Puritan*, rereading a submission—possibly in a quiet corner at the University of Toronto, where she teaches communication to budding engineers—to test the validity of her initial response. "I might read in one mood and not get it, and then read in another mood and feel differently." See her inviting a poet whose public reading she enjoyed to submit. See her revelling in a new voice, and the knowledge that she can bring it to an audience. "It's exciting—at this point *The Puritan* has so many readers—especially with a new poet, you're going to guarantee there's all these people reading their work."

And meet *Malahat* editor John Barton, who got me into all this, in the magazine's office at the University of Victoria, round a bend and up half a staircase, somewhere on the way to Medieval Studies—finding *The Malahat* feels a bit like hunting down Platform 9 ¾ to board the train to Hogwarts—preparing a set of submissions for a poetry board meeting. A portrait of *Malahat* founding editor Robin Skelton on the wall nearby, Barton is reading through readers' comments and ranking contenders. He's also slipping into "character" for the meeting. "My job," says Barton, "is to make the taste of the board bigger than it is. You are busy looking for flaws. Everything is picked apart. Sometimes we're thinking, 'This doesn't match what I'd do.' We have to get inside the poems."

Now Barton is engaging via email with a poet regarding potential tweaks to an accepted poem. In "Inside the Blind: On Editing Poetry," a talk he gave in St. John's in 2015 for the Editors Association of Newfoundland and Labrador, Barton described this as "negotiat[ing] the 'tiny shifts' that are essential to the editing of a poem… the editing of poetry at the micro level." Such work requires a delicate balance of skill and restraint. An editor must avoid leading a poet into writing the poem he or she would write. This is why Barton maintains it's more important to be a good reader than a good poet to edit the stuff. "You engage with the author's curiosity," he tells me. "The poem works when their passion becomes your passion. That means the work is alive. That means there's skill."

Finally, Barton's doing one of his favourite things: composing an acceptance letter. His tone is professional but warm. He compliments the accepted work, explaining in simple terms why it stood out. "My chief goal," says Barton, "is to participate in the author's delight. I think it's really important. We've all had the experience of a poem being published, and you barely get anything back from the editors. It's a cold experience. It's like you've found a place to warehouse your work. I try, to some extent, to participate."

To participate. This is what both poets and editors are in it for, after all—and this is one of the gifts of the literary magazine to the enterprise of literature. Not only the jolt of confidence publication brings, not just the promise of readers (however precious and marvellous)—but these joint creative adventures that take place all across the country, these productive collaborations toward clarity, heightened nuance, refined meaning.

When I became involved with *Arc* nearly two decades ago, we received submissions by mail. We sent rejections and acceptances by post. The former were standard issue, printed in the hundreds (I'd sometimes add a handwritten note.) Day-to-day correspondence was by email, but I also kept a stack of *Arc* letterhead in my home office, for more official or personalized correspondence. Now, for *Arc* and many other publications, submissions can be sent off with a few mouse-clicks, and collected in an online submission platform that logs readers' responses.

I recently dug up a spreadsheet from 2009, in which *Arc*'s managing editor recorded a total of 425 submissions. Douglas says in 2017, in January alone, 700 poems were submitted to *Arc*. *The Malahat* reports 1800 poetry submissions per year, each of which contains up to six poems. Contests boost submissions to about 2200. From the total, 70 or 80 poems make it into the magazine: less than 1 percent. By necessity, these submissions face what Barton calls "a huge triage at the beginning." Triage, depending on a publication's structure and resources, might be conducted by graduate students, interns, contributing editors, volunteer readers or staff. Someone must coordinate who has read what. Someone must log and send rejections. Someone must ready surviving submissions for the next stage of review. Amid all this administration, the basic work of publishing must also be accomplished: assigning and editing essays, reviews and interviews; design, production, proofreading and printing; budgeting, bookkeeping, bill and contributor payment; circulation, marketing, website management, contest coordination, event planning (such as launches); and the monstrous task of preparing grant applications, which resemble highly detailed multi-year business plans. Again, depending on a publication's circumstances, these tasks may be divvied up between staff and volunteers, in either case often the very same folks wading through submissions.

The first obstacle a launched poem faces is exactly what Barton pointed out to me all those years ago: crowding. By other poems, and by all the necessary work carried out *around* the poems.

Douglas, who routinely motors through 50 poems in a sitting, is conscious of the responsibility that accompanies her task, and its attendant hazards. "The hardest thing," she says, " is being read when people are reading poems one after the other. You can get lost in the rhythm." Douglas's remedy: read aloud. The impact of *hearing* the poem can't be underestimated—especially if one is reading submissions online. "It's more of a scanning kind of read. A superbly finely tuned poem with formal elements that relies on a certain subtlety in language might lose out over something that's flashier. There's a poem we see a lot of now. It has a compressed musicality that is almost similar to spoken word. It's a poem that just drives, every line drives. You can feel the voice on the screen. The poem that is quieter and more reflective definitely needs to be read aloud."

Once, at a meeting where editors were chewing over the final shortlist for *Arc*'s Poem of the Year contest—hundreds of submissions had been winnowed to 20 poems—Douglas was dead set against one of the contenders. "We're talking about a $5,000 poem. I said, flat out, God no, not this one, never this one. Then we stopped and read the poem out loud twice. And it won. I went from 'Don't embarrass me by selecting this one' to, 'That's it.'"

If it's true that submissions are plentiful, it's also true that the vast majority are weak, or, as Schott puts it, "Adequate. It's descriptive. It's OK. It's completely predicable." Most editors I spoke with expressed a longing to be surprised, to feel an inner "wow." They hope to encounter true originality, something that jolts them into a new kind of knowing. "So much of it is intuitive," says Wright. "It's something I haven't read before." We want our poetry to wake us up, to kick or even gently—but decisively—nudge us into sharper awareness. "It's a kind of treasure hunt," says Schott.

When most submissions come nowhere near resembling found treasure, frustration and even cynicism can rear. At *Arc*, during meetings in our very snug booth at Pub Italia in Ottawa—it was aptly dubbed The Confessional, and even had a little swinging door—we'd groan, for a time, over any poem incorporating Icarus. Please, dear gods, deliver us from yet another Icarus metaphor. There was something in the air: that poor burned boy had become a shortcut toward gravitas or meaning, one that came to stand in for all the absence of freshness, all the "adequate" compositions that bore no sense of urgency or of having been made from necessity. There were times I'd slogged through so many so-so submissions that I began to wonder whether my judgment was permanently impaired. The wit we traded in *Arc*'s confessional served as relief, but it was tantalizing for a reason: it was dangerous. The beleaguered poetry editor can slip into the role of slouched, weary critic: "Go on. Impress me." From here, it's a hop and a skip to disdain, and the default position of one's own taste as a bar for acceptance.

Hard truth: In the cut-throat world of publishing, even poetry editors—supposedly operating in a rare pocket of cultural purity, where the lure of profit is nonexistent—are not weighing quality alone. Collecting sets of words between covers (or on a web site) is akin to creating a contained community, a space where voices converse, echo, harmonize, clash. This is where curation comes in, a wider view that addresses considerations beyond the nature of individual poems.

Here's one example. When I worked for *Arc*, we aimed to cross-pollinate new and established voices, giving longtime writers a view of what's rising, giving those still developing their craft that esteemed company, and giving curious readers a sneak preview of up-and-comers as well as new work by known entities. This mix was elusive. Established poets often fall out of the habit of sending their work to little magazines. When they do, editors may approach their submissions with trepidation. When we spoke, Barton explained this phenomenon well: "Here you have an established poet. You're afraid you're not going to like their work. Or you're lulled into their voice, you read with past knowledge, you almost don't see the poem in front of you. It's hard to read them freshly." I suspect that, in my effort to avoid being swayed by an author's reputation, I was harder on submissions from poets who had one. On the flipside, it's exciting to feel that you've "discovered" a new voice: such discoveries are indeed a chief mandate of most lit mags.

Beyond this, some journals aim to delve deeply into a certain aesthetic. Others ambitiously seek to find and share the multiplicity of imaginative, linguistic and formal investigations underway by poets at any given time. At *The Malahat*, says Barton, "We're not reading for ourselves. We're reading for the people who pick up the magazine. The wider the range, I think the greater the readership. If someone comes and says 'I liked everything,' I've kind of failed. We're challenging the reader to step into this cold bath."

Regardless of a journal's tone or personality, I've never met an editor who dreams of homogeneity. Every reader at *The Puritan* is allowed one "veto proof" choice, in order not to lose those interesting "outliers" that Wright—who acknowledges being drawn to sonically dense poems, herself—says were being cut when decisions were wholly consensus-based. Likewise, *Puritan* sections are turned over to guest editors every summer, to allow for ranging perspectives and to encourage outreach into under-tapped constituencies. BCP's 2014 guest editor Sonnet L'Abbé took on *The Puritan*'s poetry department two years after contending with this anthology. Her preface included this reflection on a catch-22 some authors face: "Meanwhile, feminists, Black writers, and Indigenous writers working in predominantly white spaces have to negotiate their complex work being stereotyped and dismissed as 'angry,' while at the same time they may find that activist fury the only mode in which their writing is reliably recognized." The summer before, in 2015, *The Puritan*'s guest poetry editor was Métis author Katherena Vermette, who included among her choices a rich grouping of Indigenous authors, some of whose poems found their way into BCP 2016, guest edited by Helen Humphreys.

The Puritan's practice of rotating guest editors highlights a thread of curatorial concern currently stitching its way throughout Canada's lit mag scene. I can name, off the top of my head, recent or upcoming guest edited editions of three other magazines, all efforts to open doors that were previously closed or so widely perceived to be closed there was no practical difference. As part of a multifaceted, longterm effort toward what editor Pamela Mulloy calls "intentional diversity," *TNQ*'s 2017 summer issue was guest-edited by Anna Ling Kaye, a writer, journalist and former editor at Vancouver's *ricepaper* magazine. The magazine has also brought three new consulting editors into its fold to support work on regular issues—Lamees Al Ethari, Tasneem Jamal, and Alicia Elliott, a Tuscorara writer from Six Nations. Canada's 150th birthday, meanwhile, July 1, was the deadline for submissions to *Arc*'s Reconciliation, Decolonization and Nation(s) issue, guest-edited by Ojibwe poet and scholar Armand Garnet Ruffo. The call for submissions, under the heading: "Oh Canada, We Have Issues," noted that while contributions from Indigenous poets were encouraged, the call (and conversation) was open to all. In 2017, *The Malahat* published—and promptly sold out of—its Indigenous Perspectives issue, guest-edited by three Indigenous authors, one each for fiction, nonfiction, and poetry. Philip Kevin Paul took on the latter. In his introduction, he noted the thread of anger he found running through many of the submissions. "I understand this," he wrote. "The anger's still in me too. (Really?!?!? You want my perspective now?!?!?) Even at this point of my development as a poet, I find myself having to resist the temptation of just 'putting it out there.'" Having established this important context, Paul went on to discuss the craft in the poems he'd selected, including his surprise at the prevalence of rhyme, and his sense that prose poetry is a form that grows naturally from storytelling cultures.

I used to chaff at certain criticisms directed toward literary journals: those framed around power, control, and gatekeeping. That a shoestring not-for-profit lit mag with a print run of 800-1200 copies would be called powerful seemed over-the-top. Yet, as a poet, editor, and member of a literary community that can fall disappointingly short when it comes to bringing forth diverse voices, I know we can't discount the gatekeeping function of even the lowliest first reader at a small magazine. I believe literary journals are crucial: to the life of the poem, the de-isolation of the poet, and the ecosystem of poetry itself. That means how they operate, the way they make decisions, and who's involved in making those decisions—their awareness of their own subconscious biases, and potential biases—matters.

Is it optimistic to suggest that I see that awareness growing? To hope that initiatives such as those described above will spread their tendrils throughout our collective writing mind and ultimately sprout an altered literary landscape? Reviewing past editions of BCP in preparation for this anthology, Molly and I couldn't help but notice the ever-widening range of voices represented. More than one factor may contribute to this shift but, at least in part, it suggests the magazines—wellspring for all that makes its way to BCP—are changing their own composition.

How much deeper, lasting change can a few years of a poetry anthology point to? Perhaps I'm optimistic because my life experience has conditioned me to be so. Because I am white, and only now, in middle age, coming to appreciate the privilege that attribute unfairly bestows. Because we're all human, and I want to believe that beneath our dark histories and troubled politics, people are intrinsically curious, basically good. In her essay "On Seeing and Being Seen: Writing with Empathy," which appeared in the spring 2017 issue of The Writers' Union of Canada's *Write* magazine, Elliott describes the ways her literary apprenticeship has included negotiating editors' expectations. Of a certain period, she writes, "I scraped all indigeneity out of my work. At least if my fiction read as 'white' I'd be sure that any rejections were based on the work itself. I wouldn't have to yet again field questions about why my characters were Native, or deal with criticisms that they somehow weren't 'Indian enough.'" I read that and think: How unfair. Disgusting. And then I remind myself I may have biases so submerged I can't feel them acting upon me as I read. My shock at what Elliott has faced proves an innocence—or ignorance—that's just this side of complicity.

Who do I think I am? I'm a former poetry journal editor, now an anthology editor, who came into these roles unintentionally. That I've been fortunate to rise to these responsibilities under the mentorship of, first, John Barton and later, BCP's own visionary, Molly Peacock, is both lucky accident and no accident at all. Many choices, but also circumstances beyond my control, led me under their wings. We're all fortunate that the circumstances of Molly's own life led her here, to Canada, and then to a connection with the early days of Tightrope, which she rightly saw as a potential home for this annual reckoning with our ever-evolving poetic practices, and our growing and changing chorus of voices. With her wisdom, her elegance of mind, her intrinsic warmth, her deep passion for the craft, Molly has bravely ferried this vessel through the currents and rocky shoals of its first decade.

I now follow in Molly's footsteps, as well as in the footsteps of Tightrope staff, past and present. I'm also listening for the echoes of the voices of poets and speakers from all backgrounds who have walked the wilds of this tradition and this country before me. I would like to believe in a world, and more particularly in a homegrown literature, that is vital and enduring, and more than that: open, fair-minded, beyond setting up or perpetuating barriers. I would like to believe in that literature—at least that it is possible, and that we can all seek to take steps toward it. As a start, those of us in positions to weigh, consider, and choose to publish (or not) another person's writing have a responsibility to cultivate awareness of how our own perspectives may affect our responses to the work we encounter, and likewise how they may affect some writers' willingness to entrust us with their words. We must, as Mulloy wrote in a recent introduction to *TNQ*, "start with listening," especially "to those whose knowledge [comes] from an experience not our own."

This was conceived of as an essay about the journey of the poem. At the heart of that journey is the toil, passion, and care of the dozens of journal editors scattered across this vast country—this country with its tainted history and likewise imperfect present. Consider the fate of the poem—nudged from the nest, cast on the mercy of the elements, adrift without a bottle. All the possibility and uncertainty, all the pressure except the work of waiting, arrives with the poem at its destination. "Once a poem is accepted," says Barton, "it's all about respecting the text. Making sure there are no spelling errors, all the copy editing things. And helping the author realize their ambitions or hopes for their work."

We honour that passionate toil, we rely on and revel in its lush linguistic harvests, we stand gratefully knee-deep within them, hungry for more, anticipating a new growing season. May the crops rotate, reseed, renew. May they be robust. May the sun shine and the rains fall. May we all be so lucky, so blessed.

Anita Lahey
Victoria, BC

the Best of

THE Best Canadian Poetry

IN ENGLISH

TENTH
ANNIVERSARY
EDITION

MARGARET AVISON ❧

Two Whoms or I'm in Two Minds

Whenever I say, or even think:
all, launching out upon a
train of thought, then
such a clamour—
we're coming, we're about
ready, don't go without…
Without—whom?

The barley-broom in long grass
(hushed in its silken plumage),
one or two beads picked off my
childhood's dear fringed lampshade
still bright, perhaps a
vintage elm – that last
evening, in good old summertime
before the move out West (recalled
regularly by my
resolute father athirst for clear brook
water babbling over stones all deep
in blanketing snow).

How many are there
of you? Would it strike you as
better if I'd said,
"Whenever I think, or say,
everything…"?

—*thing*! What do *you* think?

All right then, that's
out, and the end
of *all* as well.

Now permit me to insist on
elaborating the thoughts I was
headed for…

You plan to do
that in
words?

      To
whom do I defer, now?

Words. Fancy,
for instance, saying that
Aplectrum hyemale (one of the
orchids) is the same as
Putty Root (its other name)!

Well, it *is* the
same plant.
Might we not both acknowledge
the borders? My
territory, the realm of truths, their
history, their
implications, and the
outworking in our ways.
                      And yours
the fields of, what?
particles?

          I like the word
particulate. Its dictionary
meaning has slipped my mind. But
do let's have a cluster of
particulates that I can
dance among, with castanets.

Peace be between and to
us, both!

from *Brick*
published in *Best Canadian Poetry 2009*

KEN BABSTOCK ℭℨ

Autumn News from the Donkey Sanctuary

Cargo has let down
her hair a little and stopped pushing
Pliny the Elder on

the volunteer labour.
During summer it was all *Pliny the Elder,*
Pliny the Elder, Pliny

the— she'd cease only
for scotch thistle, stale Cheerios, or to reflect
flitty cabbage moths

back at themselves
from the wet river-stone of her good eye. Odin,
as you already know,

was birthed under
the yew tree back in May, and has made
friends with a crow

who perches between
his trumpet-lily ears like bad language he's not
meant to hear. His mother

Anu, the jennet with
soft hooves from Killaloe, is healthy and never
far from Loki or Odin.

The perimeter fence,
the ID chips like functional cysts slipped
under the skin, the *trompe*

l'oeil plough and furrowed
field, the UNHCR feed bag and visiting
hours. These things done

for stateless donkeys,
mules, and hinnies—done in love, in lieu of claims
to purpose or rights—

are done with your
generous help. In your names. Enjoy the photo.
Have a safe winter

outside the enclosure.

from *The Fiddlehead*
published in *Best Canadian Poetry 2009*

JOHN WALL BARGER ℭ

Urgent Message from the Captain of the Unicorn Hunters

Release them. Those sealed in your attics.
Those chained in your barns. Those on the nightmare yokes.
Those heads on your walls. This was our fault.
We taught you to torture the unicorn.
That it biteth like a lion & kicketh like a horse.
That it has no fear of iron weapons.
That unicorn-leather boots ensure sound legs
& protection from plague. That unicorn liver (with a paste
of egg yolk) heals leprosy. That its tusk,
ground to dust, gives a hard-on. Forget all that.
Ye taxidermists, cut out your work.
Keep off, ye farmers of dreams & horns.
We have done enough. Baiting them with our virgins.
Cutting the heads off the calves & their mothers.
Planting birthday candles in their eyes.
Fortune-telling with their gizzards.
Tossing their balls to the dogs.—Enough!
Free them, to bathe in our rainbows.
Let them loose in their fields of sorrow.
Enough have they tholed. And you'll have to forgive:
nothing that's happened as yet
has prepared me for this. I have taken us too far
off course. Abominations, treason!
It's up to them now, our lot.
First, *let them go*. And then we wait.

from *Prairie Fire*
published in *Best Canadian Poetry 2015*

JOHN BARTON ☙

Turing's Machine

Turing believes machines think
Turing lies with men
Therefore machines do not think
      —Alan Turing, 1952

I am a computer, thinking and recording, always
Reading the fixed algorithms of the body
Codes enmeshed in the blood as literal and numeric
As they synapse through me: I lie with men and do not lie.

Reading the fixed algorithms of the body
I attempt to unlock cagy, age-old theorems of desire
As they synapse through me, I lie with men and do not lie
Alone; their primes at long last enshrined with mine.

I attempt to unlock cagy, age-old theorems of desire:
All men who shall not love are in love.
Alone, their primes at long last enshrined with mine.
Make me a machine to drowse in their arms undone.

All men who shall not love are in love
—The liar's paradox of how we must live and lie.
Make me a machine to drowse in their arms undone.
Let me record how we wake for reflection later on.

The liar's paradox of how we must live and lie.
We are ciphers none except us must ever cipher.
Let me record how we wake for reflection later on.
Who we are to those who know us not, let us try not to know.

We are ciphers none except us must ever cipher
Our tables of behaviour impregnable ones and zeros—
Who we are to those who know us not, let us try not to know
Absent from itineraries of wife and child, though we are sons.

Our tables of behaviour impregnable ones and zeros
Others allow us to join in daylight unobserved if we part
Absent from itineraries of wife and child, though we are sons
Men whose own radiant unborn will not once recode them.

Others allow us to join in daylight unobserved if we part
Ahead of logic, if we prove our circuits do not lie
Men whose own radiant unborn will not once recode them
Our undecidability exactly ours, immutable science.

Ahead of logic, if we prove our circuits do not lie
We are a subroutine Sparta's sacred band first posed
Our undecidability exactly ours, immutable science
This lying together configured to a repeating future.

We are a subroutine Sparta's sacred band first posed
Codes enmeshed in the blood as literal and numeric
This lying together configured to a repeating future.
I am a computer, thinking and recording always.

from *The Literary Review of Canada*
published in *Best Canadian Poetry 2011*

SHIRLEY BEAR ❧

Flight

on this rooftop of 1000 parker street is a frozen lake
empty now
the ducks have flown south
and the geese are in victoria island, probably at the
butchart gardens
today january 16 2000
winter rains in vancouver have created a frozen lake
on the rooftop
outside my studio and my
memories follow you to the water's edge
watch as you test the water
my mind's eye etches
this provocative musical moment
into my soul my body anticipates
as it interprets your penetrating gaze
are you here or is it only my fantasy staring back
your invitation has flown away
I gaze at the gray frozen lake and remember
a flowing river and
I am transported
to a time where returning becomes at once impossible
I have walked with you forever
in the valleys of time and space
by the rivers of ever-flowing
where the sun melted
the icy rooftops of memory
watched as you poured the river
down your bodyscape
etching pathways
like rain on the window pane
making its way
slowly to the apex
the birds have taken flight
and nature has imprinted their image on
this frozen rooftop lake

from *West Coast LINE*
published in *Best Canadian Poetry* 2009

YVONNE BLOMER ☙

The Roll Call to the Ark

               Was it that He said a pair
was it that He said seven pairs
               If it was a pair
if it was seven pairs
               Then what of those un-hatched
what of those fledglings
               What of inbreeding
souls and souls of silent sameness
               If it was a pair
if it was seven pairs
               Then let's start here
start with the lesser tit, the bearded
               With the Golden Eagle, the Imperial
does He care how they are named
               Does He care if they are beautiful
He does
               They are
the sparrow
               The Griffon Vulture
the golden oriole
               The Peregrine
does He care how they stand
               So proud, such long thin necks
so small, such plumage
               The Hoopoe, The Snow
finch, the skylark
               Did His friend gather
the eggs of the robin, the dove
               Crow, Raven eggs
did he eat any of them
               Did he crack them over a fire
feed them to his sons
               Feed them to his sons' wives
and how did he house them
               In the ribs of a cypress
in an aviary of dream

                        For the Little Owl
for the tree pipit
                        Did he take the seeds of trees
did he take branches
                        Foliage
some arching trunk
                        Was it crowded with still eyes
was it loud with tweets and twitters and tittering
                        Did the sons
did the wives
                        Threaten to hunt
yell out amid eternal headaches
                        How
how
                        Did they gather
that small-winged
                        Those sharp-clawed
the goldcrest
                        The Fisher-Owl
and what did they eat
                        Did he build a lake
did he build a forest
                        Did he let them out
did they feed on fruit
                        Clean the flooded lands
clean the fly-laden tables
                        Of the ripening flesh
of the overripe rinds and cores
                        Did He ponder
did He consider
                        The length and breadth
the tiny-ness
                        Of The Harpy Eagle
the bee humming bird
                        Its taller-than-man wing span
its eggs smaller than the smallest finger nail
                        Its potential to catch up
its potential to hide
                        Did He consider
did He ponder

Hand-sized talons
all the tiny hiding places
Claws the length of a grizzly's
the arctic tern's yearly flight around the world?

from *Descant*
published in *Best Canadian Poetry 2008*

STEPHANIE BOLSTER ☙

Gardening

Under the foxgloves, worms. A white
gleam writhes, cut, under the shovel.

What I doubled multiplies down there
below what I thought I made good.

from *Branch*
published in *Best Canadian Poetry 2012*

TIM BOWLING ❧

Union Local 64

Last night I caught the boy I'd been
in fishnet and gutted him
on the government wharf
by the light of an oil lamp
hung from my dead father's hand.

Above the dyke, over the road,
the town was just the same:
weeping willows, widows,
whalestains on the cheesecloth walls
of the first houses
and an overwhelming sense
of a last breath being taken.

The worst of it was
the ordinary blood
on the ordinary wood
and my father saying
as he gazed out to sea
"It's no good.
The companies won't pay.
They didn't pay for mine
and they won't pay for yours."

I watched him through my mother's eyes
as he sighed and bent
to the stiffened body of our time
together not worth one red cent
to anyone and picked it up
and took his life and mine away again.

from *The Fiddlehead*
published in *Best Canadian Poetry 2011*

ASA BOXER ☙

Dante's Ikea

In the bedrooms of Ikea-land,
where love's theatres are assembled,
my sweetheart wept

upon the softest bed. I'd scoffed,
insisted I could neither rest nor play
upon these stock sarcophagi.

We shuffled over to Living Rooms
and sat on separate couches, neither one
prepared to pay unbeatable prices.

We drifted to kitchens sharpened
knives, tested chopping blocks, drew
close, imagining winter-roasts and wine.

But the pepper-mills were plastic
and the wood was melamine.
We dared not taste the fruits.

With hearts in throat, we headed down
to the second circle. There, a horde
of howling children caged in glass.

Smiling wryly at my companion,
I queried why they balled their eyes out so.
And answering somberly, she replied:

"They wail so because their parents
have lied to them again about the time.
Another eternity has passed them by!"

The toilets and the urinals hissed
just down the hall, but none emerging
came to claim these orphaned babes.

Feeling they ought to know,
I volunteered that mum and dad were lost
among the boxes down below.

At which they turned their red-eyed
demon-faces, and stoned my image
in the glass with hollow plastic balls.

From thence we proceeded till
we stood atop the stairwell to the final
warehouse floor, and there, we paused

and thus we prayed: "Dear God,
I hope the pieces fit this time."
Then down we tread

to the third, most dreaded circle;
and with each awful step,
we took the holy name.

The pillows brought no comfort.
The bathmats were all wrong.
The candles smelled like poison.

The vases lacked all grace of form.
The picture-frames and hangers,
though, were irresistible.

Further in, the daunting stacks
of all that we'd been shown above.
The boneyard of domesticity,

where bits and pieces of living
lie in boxes like the dead.
Billies, Nannas, Ivars and Johans

stacked on scrap-wood pallets.
What if Robin's legs and Markor's screws
were mixed with Mikael's top?

"Dare we crack it open?
Look inside? Is it gauche
to show a lack of faith down here?"

"I don't care," she answered,
"nothing matters any more." It seemed
we'd found the fabled vale of despair.

And just beyond, awash with sun!
—O blessed sun!—Hope.
You are meant to see the light

and stand within a few short metres
of that happy plain we call the parking lot.
With eyes asquint, you can spot

your car. But by Zeno's law, the line
you're in is an infinite series of half-steps,
halves of half-steps, halves of those.

A twisting child, red and raw with sobbing,
entangled in a wire cart-seat, shrieked
and blew green bubbles from her nose.

At the checkout, we surrendered our identities,
signed our names away; then wheeled off,
beyond the glaring exit-doors.

from *Arc Poetry Magazine*
published in *Best Canadian Poetry 2009*

JULIE BRUCK ❦

Two Fish

Say you have two goldfish, pet-store
fishlets bought for 25 cents each, carried
home in a plastic bag and nurtured for years.
Let's say you clean the tank, place each fish
in its own half-filled Mason jar, each
a bit small for large fish, but adequate
for the short time it should take to balance
the tank's pH. Suppose you put the jars on a very
high shelf, then forget they're there for months,
until most of the water has evaporated, until
what's left of the fish-shapes surrenders
to the dictates of the jars, becoming two squat
cyphers of twisted life. Let's say that's how
you find them, your heart swelling with shame,
and quickly, with shaking hands, pour them
back into the tank. Which is more alarming?
The fish who sinks to the bottom, distorted
as in a funhouse mirror, one eye bulging
to the size of its chest, fins extruding
from the wrong places, who squats there
staring out, steady as a barrel? Or the one
who reconstitutes itself as a sponge takes
on tap water, who swims off briskly,
picking up and dropping bits of gravel
with its fish lips, foraging with little
clicks, as it always did before? Which?
The hideously damaged one, or the one
who moves on as if this was what it meant
to be entrusted to your care? Which fish?

from *Hazlitt*
published in *Best Canadian Poetry 2015*

ANNE CARSON ❧

Father's Old Blue Cardigan

Now it hangs on the back of the kitchen chair
where I always sit, as it did
on the back of the kitchen chair where he always sat.

I put it on whenever I come in,
as he did, stamping
the snow from his boots.

I put it on and sit in the dark.
He would not have done this.
Coldness comes paring down from the moonbone in the sky.

His laws were a secret.
But I remember the moment at which I knew
he was going mad inside his laws.

He was standing at the turn of the driveway when I arrived.
He had on the blue cardigan with the buttons done up all the way to the top.
Not only because it was a hot July afternoon

but the look on his face—
as a small child who has been dressed by some aunt early in the morning
for a long trip

on cold trains and windy platforms
will sit very straight at the edge of his seat
while the shadows like long fingers

over the haystacks that sweep past
keep shocking him
because he is riding backwards.

from *Brick*
published in *Best Canadian Poetry 2013*

PETER CHIYKOWSKI ☙

Notes from the Canary Islands

Four weeks off the coast, crotch rotting
in seawater, cock cupped
by the wetsuit,
and I swear to God
I'd marinate a whale
in petroleum just to see
your face again.
I hate how the satellite phone
spits oil in my ear
when we try to talk,
how the ocean throbs under me
like a toe
stubbed. All
in the name
of research.

The bureau says it takes 22 gallons of oil
to manufacture a truck tire,
which helps me understand
the ritual waste of repeating
I miss you,
and
I miss you,
and
I miss you,
to be heard just once
above the cackle of static.

I think that somewhere
between our shores
swims a giant sea turtle
choke-chained by telephone wires,
muzzled by envelopes,
gulping up those stray *I miss you*'s.
One day he'll wash up on a beach,
rot out a bellyful of our words
for all the world to smell. I think about

the carcasses of our conversations,
know our love must end up
somewhere, must ooze its way
to some lonely reef
and make one fish
the happiest in all the sea.

Shouting to be heard above
the buzz of salt and shaky cables
makes for poor conservation,
but let the ocean have its slurry of words;
the world could stand to be polluted
by a little more
unnecessary love.

from *Grain*
published in *Best Canadian Poetry 2011*

GEORGE ELLIOTT CLARKE ❧

A Letter from Henry Tucker, August 28, 1789

I

Arrowing from Bermuda—
"Isle of Devils"
(whose rocks and reefs wreck ships)—
right after the Equinox,
and veering to Nova Scotia,
skirting the Leeward Isles,
I was strengthened in my persuasion
that Bermuda is a "sea-garden,"
a tropical England,
a "Summer Island,"
except that sly types hold the government tiller,
and plunge pirate hands in the public till,
shouting "Free Trade" in slaves
(for they are dissatisfied with profits
from salt and Madeira wine),
and do resort to any pulpit-fraud,
(their piety echoing thunderously),
to seize whatever riches
from whomever
in whatever way…

I'll forget these woes.
I have one dream—
to kiss my daughter,
to have my wife again…

II

I met them, out of Ireland,
off Newfoundland,
and my sweet darling Mrs. Tucker,
surprised by my bronze, Bermudian complexion,
exclaimed to our excited daughter,
"That's *not* your papa, Nellie!
That's a Coloured man!"

22

She was assured of her error
in our evening intimacy,
and her face shot pure crimson,
while I guffawed like a Bedlam madman:
"Oh, how can a white ever be black?"

III

On to Halifax—inclement town,
we came,
to streets parading snow and sleighs,
the sound of a million puny church bells tinkling—
as cheery Christians slid (or backslid,
blaming ice,
not *Vice*).

The British soldiers looked like Finns—
furred in beaver at the head
and in buffalo to the toe.

The Haligonian houses and wharves—
all wood—
await a match
to render them Xmas candles.
I'm sure they'll not wait long:
Halifax is as favoured with fires
as it is with blizzards.

Our Nova Scotian stay was only loss and loss.
We explored a salt-and-vinegar world—
miserable with slush and caustic with ice
and dirty.
(*Love* itself was covert there:
the streets churned up urchins and sluts.)
Opinions proved as provincial as indigestion.

IV

After weeks of cold that needled us worse
than Bermuda's mosquitoes
(whose bites whelp blisters as big as buckles),
we set out for our "Devil's Summer Island,"

but got pitched and bitched in the North Atlantic—
a merciless ocean.
We could not gain softer latitudes quickly enough.

(At night, the black-face ocean was lit
only by stingy stars;
the light was dingy…)

We took the "wine of height"
as soon as was possible,
downing port-and-cheese by candlelight,
salted by the sea.

Not too long after Sable Island,
we reached our realm feeling blessed
(save for the Yellow Fever
that floats in with the Southern cotton).

V

Now we have darkies,
and Nova Scotia has darkies,
and we all have Christ.
And we all split "fair" from "dark."
But no one cares for the Nova Scotian Negroes,
despite the black-robed, long-coat traffic
of clergy twixt Halifax (NS) and Hamilton (BDA),
with white Believers assisting brown Bermudians,
but ignoring New Scotland's scruffy blacks.

It seems *Salvation* is segregated too.

But we shouldn't wonder.

Must slaves have souls?

[Southampton (Bermuda) 30 mars MMXII]

from *Canadian Literature*
published in *Best Canadian Poetry 2014*

DON COLES ∽

Memory, Camus, Beaches

In his *Carnets* Camus notes that his memory
isn't what it used to be, hence his
emotional life, "devoid of the long echo
that memory gives," has diminished.
A typically Camusian admission, lifted
above normal discourse in the way
all his best pages are, by a moment of
pure crystal—that "long echo,"

Which is interesting, but not blown-away
interesting. So, a re-start and a circling-back.
Psychiatrists are currently saying that we take
near-permanent note of every sight and sound
our lives offer us, filing away not only casual
scenes and events (and lately, from abandoned
hangars and unsupervised outbuildings,
the shredded, corridor-strewn contents of
once-cloistered, now Googleable, libraries both
ancient and modern), but also fierce angers,
immense joys, summer TV re-runs and NFL
hi-lites, in short whatever's now going or once went.
All this stacks up in our head-mass,
most of it seemingly lost in there but all,
apparently, retrievable if we can catch even fleeting
glimpses of it. Glimpses from which may come
limitless things.

Think about it! But not for long, because we have
much else to consider.

Camus. We left him a while ago but now we're
back. He's OK with it. A few years ago I
walked into a military cemetery near Arras
with my son, and guess what was
the first name we saw on one of those
modest little tablets the French have for
their war dead. Same for all of them, by

the way, officers, NCOs, *poilus*—no distinction
of rank, everybody under the durable rubric
Mort pour la Patrie. But no, the dead one's name
was *not* 'Camus,' although I don't blame you
for the guess. It was 'Lévesque,' the surname of
a charmless landlady I had in Quebec one summer
when I was 19 and really liked a girl called Lorna,
a "plain" girl, somebody told me she was,
warning me off, I suppose, or trying to, but
as things have turned out, one of only six or seven
remembered women on whose faces light can still fall,
still stubborn for happiness. Which reminds me
that Stendhal, visiting London in 1820,
recorded in his diary his admiration for the way
Englishwomen walked in the streets "so scantily clad,
the breasts of plain girls shaking like jelly."

NB, the long reach of a plain word.

The next name, the very next one, was Camus.
Just that, no extras.

I have asked myself: did Camus, Albert, come to
his 'long echo' while working in his wisdom-stuffed
Paris study, or did it arrive unasked during
one of his walks along the endless sea-fronts and
white-sand beaches of Algiers?

It's exactly such matters that I'd like to get
clarity on! Best not to fret, I know that,
but just one more thing while we're here.
Camus's novels, especially the short ones, especially
my all-time favourite, *La Chute*, which brims
with sadness, so much so that to speak of it
extensively here would capsize the poem—
what about it, or them? (Here's a scene from
La Chute, but *un*extensive, almost all nouns
unmodified). A man's walking across
one of the Seine bridges in Paris on a foggy day
and passes behind a young woman leaning over
the railing and seeming to stare down at

the river. He feels as a man always feels passing by
a woman who's standing quietly alone anywhere—
that is, a pang of loss. A minute later, having
walked on, he hears a cry, and pauses, and
hears the cry repeated several times, the sound
coming from farther away, growing fainter, and
ceasing...

You see? It's obvious how all this could capsize.

He was the world's most glamorous postwar writer,
for his perfectly-timed postwar novels and essays
as well as for being (which isn't always the case with
writers of either sex) mentionably handsome,
two circumstances not unrelated to his becoming
the lover of a number of admired women, among these
the seriously beautiful film and stage actress
Maria Casarès, daughter of a Spanish Prime Minister
and the woman with whom Camus, as a matter of record,
spent the night of D-Day partying, a party from which
the two of them returned, even while the Normandy beaches
known as Omaha and Gold and Juno were still lit-up and lethal,
"by bicycle, a bit drunk, with Maria riding on the handlebars."

He was killed in a car crash on the Côte d'Azur,
only 47 years old. Where could he have gone,
what could he have done, if he had lived longer?
He could only have fallen. *La Chute*. An exceptional
fall, it would have been, because a fall from
exceptional favour.

When I, unaware of the day's significance,
was walking in my usual meaningless way
down Kungsgatan, the main street of Stockholm,
first saw him, with his wife beside him, seated
in the back of the limo which was driving
the two of them towards the ceremony in
the Royal Palace, *Kungliga Palatsen*, at which
the King of Sweden would give him his Nobel Prize,
neither of them looking to one side or the other, hence
neither ever noticing what at first so startled and then

greatly moved me—startled, because it was so
unrehearsed, it came about so naturally and even so
naively—namely, that the pedestrians who had been
walking near me all came to a stop, to a sudden stillness,
the men doffing their hats and both men and women
bowing their heads as the limo slowly passed—
I was so moved by what I was seeing, this unbidden
reverence shown to a mere writer (nothing 'mere'
about him but still, a writer), that I failed to bow.
Not bowing, I watched him as long as I could,
and for as long as I saw him he was staring ahead,
gloomily.

I wanted to have 'despairingly' there, a deeper and
darker adverb for sure, a word to end a poem on,
but it kept on looking false. I'd have needed to be
closer.

from *The Fiddlehead*
published in *Best Canadian Poetry 2011*

ANNE COMPTON ❧

Stars, Sunday Dawn

> *Declination: the angular distance of a star, north or south of a celestial marker.*

Mornings, the boy is down the stairs before he knows it. The body
  leading.
A banister of hours beneath his hands. Habit has no need of light in
  halls—
above, below—the width of oriental runners. Their import worn—
  ravelled
by the circuit he's made of every surface. Each room, a perimeter of
  breath.

Blur of tartan over the newel post, rakish skid, and he's where I wait:
parlour, window-starting bright—glazed trees and beyond a band
of violet clouds girdling the horizon—stars paling on a victor's belt.

All this he sees, ignores,
                the spinning boy, my brother,
                            for whom the day's a stadium.

The granary—I need you to see this—an amphitheatre of yellow
  chaffy light.
The bins of grain are up the wooden stairs; the crusher's chute, the
  only thing below.
Where wagons wait, or will, when day is fully come. Bran or
  middlings,
depending on the setting of the gears. Grinding days, all but Sunday.
A wall calendar for figuring, tacked on a two-by-four. The planets in
  their courses

It's here, he explains the dividend of seconds; sometimes, the
  escapement of a watch.
Too young to read, I'd read its face a hundred times, and his—its
  fractional fury every dawn.
Lapsed time, he says, equates to distance: start to finish. Flight of
  thought between.
He's got his helmet hat on, the ear flaps tied behind like usual.
                            Its leather cracked with time.

A declination, I think, is what I'd name it now, that interval from
    there to here.

For some, the poem's a timepiece, a repeater watch. The one who
    watches
hauls out of harm's way a Sunday boy who hadn't breath for common
    days.

from *The Malahat Review*
published in *Best Canadian Poetry 2008*

DANI COUTURE ❧

Salvage

You can tell a thousand-footer
by her straight back, hammer head
—a skyscraper toppled.
Too long for locks, what she's best at:
pushing taconite from Duluth to Gary,
the endless circuitry of ports.
Built from the centre of the earth up,
this ship is a piece of ceremonial armour,
a leviathan penny, a horseshoe
pinned to Great Lakes lucky until she's not.
Christened and kissed off
years before you were born,
she is an older sister, a summer cousin
who only appears in a quarter of your photos
and out of focus. She's your favourite
because you barely know her.
In smaller water, this ship could be
an island, bridge, or territory.
She is a herd of 20,000 horses
trembling to shake off its load.
In her wake, lesser vessels are sent to scrap,
run aground, and peeled down to air, yet one day
it will cost less to wreck her than to keep her:
a final trip to Port Colborne or Alang.
Breakers will scrabble up her hard-rusted sides,
pull her down by torch and hand.
Her pieces soon held in the gut
of another ship downbound for better things.

After the Edwin H. Gott

from *The Walrus*
published in *Best Canadian Poetry 2012*

LUCAS CRAWFORD ❧

Failed Séances for Rita MacNeil (1944-2013)

> *We are all*
> *the weary travellers*
> *Travelling travelling on*
>   —Rita MacNeil

I

Rita, you requested that your ashes
be held in a teapot—"two if necessary"
Low days, I browse plus-size caskets
(They are all pink or blue)
But you took death with milk and sugar, long steep
    Rita, we are both members of the fat neo-Scottish diaspora.
    Don't tell me it doesn't exist, sweet darlin'
    until you are the only fat transsexual
    at a Rankin Family concert in Montreal.
    Until you feel more at home than you have all year
    when Raylene (1960-2012) thumbs-ups
    your 400-pound dance moves in the front row
    during that last, last, encore.
        Fare thee well, love.
        Will we never meet again no more?

II

In Grade Two, I sang with your coal mining choir, "The Men of the Deeps"
There is something terrifying about one-hundred pre-pubescent squirts
squeaking out the high falsetto tones of "We Rise Again"
over the miners' sea of too-knowing bass tones.

The highest note of the song comes at the word "child"
and we screamed it. We didn't yet have the sadness
that keeps you from even trying the high notes in that tune,
which take you from ours to other worlds and back again.

One of the miners comes forward in concerts for a mustachioed solo
I heard him on the CBC the day you died, having an open cry
They all wear helmets onstage. They are all Henny Penny
ever hardhat-ready for another falling sky.

Rita, did I ever tell you my great uncle Miley died in the mines?
My mother and I drove to Glace Bay last year
The old company houses are split down the middle
Each half is a different hand-painted hue and empty

We bowled candlepin alone in the basement of a church
It did not strike us to genuflect upon entry

III
Rita, I heard the RCMP trailed you in the '70s!
They were not good Arts reviewers, those Mounties:

*She's the one who composes and sings women's lib songs. 100 sweating,
uncombed women standing around in the middle of the floor with their arms
around each other crying sisterhood and dancing.*

They didn't know the *gravitas* required of a fat woman with a microphone.
They didn't see you as a teenager with a baby decades before *Juno*
Or the surgeries you had for cleft palate in your youth
Not even the abuse you sang through

They don't believe in ghosts like we do or know those family spirits
that can refill a rum tumbler when your back is turned.

IV
Rita, do you remember the "Heritage" commercial about mine collapse?
An actor swears that they sang those hymns
Even drank their own *you know*

At seven, this frightened me
But now I've seen a bit
I've watched Ashley MacIsaac (1975–) discuss urination during sex
I still toe-tap to his first crossover hit
Still watch the bit on Conan O'Brien
where Ashley kicks up his kilt
while going commando.
Yes, to queer kids watching at home
a kilt can become a portal to another life
not yet witnessed or understood.
Step we gaily, on we go!

Heel for heel and toe for toe!
I want to feel him move his bow, dab at his brow,
wash his feet, or at least buy him a pedicure
so that I can tell him that the queer, rural Nova Scotian diaspora
      (don't tell me it doesn't exist, b'y)
needs him to survive because
my accent is buried in Banff now
and he's the last member of my trinity still,
last I checked, alive.

V
One of my fat aunts resembles you, Rita.
Once, at the liquor store, someone cried:
I didn't know that you're in town for a show!
My aunt grabbed her rye and tried to smile
She drove home angry foot to floor
had her niece pour the spirit
until the ice would float.

Now she's on the wagon.
Her niece is a nephew.
Things change, Rita.

      Rita, say anything! Tell me we can break biscuits
      with blueberries and Devonshire cream.

      Say that you'll let pitch-free me
      hum along as you sing me to sleep.

      Just don't tell me we didn't exist
      Don't tell me you don't

                feel the same way too

from *Room*
published in *Best Canadian Poetry 2015*

LORNA CROZIER ◌

Seeing My Father in the Neighbours' Cockatoo

The cockatoo says three things:
"Cookie," "Pretty bird," and
"What a beautiful day!"
Some mornings you don't want to hear,
"What a beautiful day!"
but nothing stops him.

His name is Joey. Perhaps because
he wants to be something other
than a bird, he pulls the feathers
from his breast,
his grey and naked skin
what you glimpse between
an old man's buttons.

This trick does much
to make him unattractive
though he's a friendly bird, quite
beautiful when he lifts the yellow
plume on the top of his head.

If you say, "Kiss, Joey, kiss,"
and stroke his feathered cheek,
he'll bunt your hand like a cat
and click his beak. Sometimes
when he's feeling fond he'll curl
his tongue, a thick black snake,
around your finger.

The day my father decides to come back,
he hovers behind Joey's eyes
and looks at me in that way he had,
as if he'd left us long before he died
to find a new religion,
or grow cell by cell
into a different species,
tired of his memories, the tumours

in his throat that made him sound
as if he shouted underwater.

No matter how I listened
I could not understand
what he was trying to say.

Now in Joey's voice he cries
"What a beautiful day!"
and looks straight at me,
his eyelids grey and wrinkled.
Then with a wink,
he plucks three feathers from his chest
and lets them fall.

from *The Windsor Review*
published in *Best Canadian Poetry 2011*

MICHAEL CRUMMEY C3

Minke Whale In Slo-mo

A dark patch of ocean blisters up near
the gunwale with alien deliberation,

sea-water on the rising surface crackling
and receding like celluloid snared in

a projector's heat before the grappling
hook of the dorsal fin enters the frame,

pinning the shapeless shape to a name,
to identifiable attributes and traits,

the yellow dory jarred by the collision
then rocking back as the minke shears

down and away and disappears
like a drunk driver fleeing a minor

accident through backroads, deserted streets.
Repeat the thirty-second clip a dozen

times for the little mystery's slow motion
resolve, for that rough kiss so impulsive

and unexpected it leaves the diminutive
wooden boat shaking on the ocean.

from *Arc Poetry Magazine*
published in *Best Canadian Poetry 2013*

KAYLA CZAGA ❧

That Great Burgundy-Upholstered Beacon of Dependability

Over dinner, my landlady laughs about her day
teaching rich Korean kids the difference
between nightstand and one-night stand.
Her son goes wild for the bicycle pump.
From his high chair, he wails for it, erupting
borscht. Two years old and he refuses to sit
without its hard plastic denting his chin.
I don't get relationships. Once I got lace
panties in the mail from a friend who lives
in Winnipeg. He wrote, *I'm coming to visit
you at Christmas!* So I spent December
avoiding him, pretending to be busy, ice-skating
until my feet purpled, wondering how love
could transpire so oppositely between two
people. My mother once loved a grey van
so completely she sat in it for twenty minutes
every winter morning while it defrosted.
They listened to the radio together, to her
favourite tapes. The van went everywhere
with her, unlike my father who plays poker.
It lived for thirteen years in our driveway,
a great burgundy-upholstered beacon
of dependability, until its engine went.
I want to climb into you and strap myself
in, but that's not really love. Instead,
we idle in separate uncertainties, exhausting
reassurances. You thank my landlady
for dinner and roll away into a night
that imperfectly intersects my own, and I try
to stop imagining the ways we could fail
each other, and the people in rooms
everywhere who are continually failing
each other, and hope towards someday
having one nightstand with you, maybe two.

from *The Fiddlehead*
published in *Best Canadian Poetry 2015*

MARY DALTON ✂

A Little Tin Pail

The notes abandon so much as they move,
and now it is the souring flowers of the bedraggled,
alone by the river with its mandolin.

And the young ones?
And another man, who remains inside his own house,
throwing a little tin pail at the heart of the priest.

On either side there's a wall
that holds up the huge doors and altars;
the screen door bangs and it sounds so funny—

the green-headed fly shouts as it buzzes past,
watching the landscape unravel into what's gone.
The ant's a centaur in his dragon world,

but when he finds that thin green seed,
branches agog with secrecies
that spring—

maybe he didn't make it. Maybe hydrogen—
people believe it, maybe from laziness.
And to participate with the flayer.

On a misshapen wheel
we play "What animal would you be?"
It must swim for miles through the desert,

the rocks,
the bestiaries of the ancients—
speechless with soil, and blind.

from *Riddle Fence*
published in *Best Canadian Poetry 2010*

SADIQA DE MEIJER ✑

Exhibit

This is the pink salwar kameez she made for me.
Here are the airmailed measurements.
Shoulder width and ankle cuffs. Blurred fingers
sewing sequins on slipping fabric.

This is my scowl in the photograph.
These upstairs bathroom fixtures are a witness
to arms in bleaching cream and the straw
of winter fields is my landscape.

Salwar kameez over heavy boots.
Salwar kameez as comet between car and banquet hall,
trail of rosewater coconut chemical blister.
That was on manual shutter-speed.

Here is my face in a hundred miniscule mirrors,
compound eye of classmates, strangers, satellites
and drones are cratering
my countries, I haven't been there.

This is the sale-priced rayon and here
is my pain threshold. Salwar kameez as costumes
on the thrift store's rack with zombie leotards
and skeletons on coat hangers.

This seam fastens sleeves to skin and the trajectory
of freefall was impossible to document
because of snow. Salwar kameez as nakedness.
Salwar kameez as parachute.

from *The Fiddlehead*
published in *Best Canadian Poetry 2014*

BARRY DEMPSTER ☙

Groin

Drop your drawers, doctor-talk, making me
feel like a dresser stuffed with wrinkled shirts
and clumps of socks. Inhuman to be
naked here, Calvin Kleins twisted around my ankles.
An X-rated cartoon, a bare-assed platypus.
Turns out I'm also swollen lymph glands,
a groin bulging with the need for attention.
It all started with an infected tooth, but that's
not important as I stretch out on the table
like luncheon meat. I'm breeze where breeze
rarely goes, new hands lifting and squeezing,
fingers joined together in a tiny oh. I'm a startled
glow, a testicle pearling with fluorescent light,
surrendering its eggy code of secrecy.
Beyond dirty thoughts, further out than
erections can reach, a strange tenderness
softly prickles, pores exhaling, saggy and sallow
smoothing their entanglements. This *is* human
after all, a scrutiny that only love can muster:
          the desire to really know.
I lie there, held, seen, wondered, as we talk
about the marvels and mishaps I've always been.

from *Canadian Literature*
published in *Best Canadian Poetry 2009*

JERAMY DODDS ❧

The Gift

The streets flooded by people watching an apartment fire.
The Klu Klux white dress she wore. The weather's rigmarole.
The silver hero in the clouds. The galvanizing. The franchise.
The bright backwash. The hollow village. The weather's rebuttal.
The throat-cut rooster, its beak wide with crow.
The mule train bringing a piano through scrub-brush.
The dwarf pines. The winterkill. The birch-knots in the stove.
The waft as souvenir. The ripe lanterns in the orchard.
The crinoline lakes. The drowned lollystick legs.
The fishnets. The doldrums. The wanderlust. The Duchess.
The gramophone's tin ear. The carriage road.
The leaf mould. The unexploded ordinance. The bloom.
The small arms fire. The child fire. The sightlines.
The dooryard. The courtlight. The wraith-sparrows.
The swagger. The little something to cut the dust.
The carbines. The Admirals niece in oilskins.
The understudy who runs away with his wife.
The regency. The deadweight. The bedside telephone.
The stairs down the bluffs. The Empress on the pebble beach.
The moulting snakes. The wildfowl. The caverns.
The names run down by their echo.
The piano so immaculate it must be hollow.
The hawthorn belt around her muslin dress.
The jackdaws. The peck horns. The silverfish.
The dust-dulled brass. The rabbit-punch.
The wicker traps. The overcoat gone to seed.
The boozy weave of a grackle off the pane.
The same thin richness of these worlds remain.
The cavalcade along her legs. The coronation.
The cannonade of hailstones on the xylophones.
The pterodactyl of silence that follows.

[* The italicized line is from Peter Porter's poem "John Marston Advises Anger".]

from *Arc Poetry Magazine*
published in *Best Canadian Poetry 2008*

GLEN DOWNIE ☙

Nocturnal Visitors

They're not fooling anyone with those Lone Ranger masks, a disguise as thin as Clark Kent's glasses. But they're super with their hands—opening garbage cans, unwrapping fish guts—believe me, you don't know the half. They climbed down our tree one night while we were eating. My watch was drying on the picnic table after slipping off into the punch. Mom took it apart *in the dark* and licked its gears clean while her babies tied my shoelaces together. It keeps better time now than it ever did—a bit slow in the day, but always sharp at night. It's only the 9 to 5 that keeps them out of dentistry and the bomb squad. With the right piano, Chopin would be a breeze.

from *Exile*
published in *Best Canadian Poetry 2010*

SUSAN ELMSLIE ☙

Box

Big enough for me to crawl into. It might've held
a fake Christmas tree, neighbour's TV or holiday
imperishables from the Sally Ann.
I was ten, making a house in the living room.

Cut out a window, opened a door. "Look at my box"
I called to my mother, and her friend put down his drink,
chided, half-slurred, "Don't say that," in a tone
that begged me to ask why. "Don't say

that" he said again. And in the pause
while he raised his glass in slow-mo and drank,
eyeing me, I sat back on my heels and glimpsed
the fourth wall, a spare self watching a trashy play.

"Cut it out" my mother said, "she's just a kid," swatting
the wasp after the sting. "I'm just a fucking drunk," his line.
Everything doubled, obscene, sublime—
No safety in words, then. And more room.

from *Arc Poetry Magazine*
published in *Best Canadian Poetry 2008*

RAOUL FERNANDES ଔ

White Noise Generator

for Amanda Todd

The autumn air feels guilt, the trees feel guilt, the cables
and the pixels, the birds and the ditch. A tornado forms,
tries to suck a ghost back down from its slow lift. Fails,
then roars through the town then toward the next town
over. Makes a point to hit every billboard on the way.

Horses run through sea-foam, white horses running
through a calendar. The cold chemical smell of a
permanent marker squeaking over rectangles of
paper. A mood-ring on her hand rotating through the
spectrum. All the strength needed in the narration, the
thorn that digs deeper with the telling. What happened
and is happening and the strength needed still.

Friend request like a conch shell left on your doorstep.
Friend request like devil-horning every face in my old
yearbook while on the phone into the wee hours. Friend
request like would you like to see the portal I found in
the school's darkroom? Friend request like let's cover
ourselves in wet leaves and mud before math class.
Friend request like I'll be your white noise generator.

An ocean is a good listener. An ocean works the teen
suicide hotline 24-7 throughout the year. A conch shell
(stay with me) is a telephone.

Friend request like a poem typed in an empty chat-room
at the end of the night. Friend request like I got a rooftop,
a joint, and a handful of stars with your name on it.
Friend request like what is difficult is what is necessary
is what is actually listening to another human speaking.

Picture a pear tree in the middle of a wasteland where the
pear tree is you and the wasteland is the comment section.

Never interrupt a girl while she is trying to draw a
horse. Never laugh when she whisper-sings under her
breath walking across the soccer field. She may be
summoning dragons, she may be summoning them
against you.

Flashcards held in front of a window. Another then
another. Trust and we shall be the receiver; love and
we shall be the amplifier. Until the amplifier short
circuits, the windows blow out, and silence splashes
everywhere.

from *subTerrain*
published in *Best Canadian Poetry 2015*

SAMUEL GARRIGÓ MEZA ❦

Capture Recapture

Each bear was marked with a numbered metal tag in one or both ears. Each bear was tagged with a numbered tag in each ear, and a plastic tag in one ear for subsequent identification. Each bear was tagged with numbered aluminium ear tags and tattooed with a corresponding number in the right ear and upper lip. Each bear was assigned a unique number printed on a set of ear tags and tattooed to the left and right sides of the upper lip. Each bear was tattooed with an identification number in the upper lip and tagged in each ear with a numbered, colour coded tag. Each bear was tagged with a Monel metal cattle tag and a red nylon rototag in each ear, with identical numbers on all four tags. Each bear was fitted with a MOD-500 radio-collar equipped with a mortality sensor and cotton spacers. Each bear was fitted with a satellite telemetry collar and equipped with a VHF radiotransmitter in the 151 MHz range. Each bear was tattooed on the upper inside lip and had uniquely numbered ear tags attached to both ears.

from *The Capilano Review*
published in *Best Canadian Poetry 2013*

MICHELLE GOOD ❦

Defying Gravity

So many rivers we wandered without helmsman or guide.
   Some so shallow the stones barely below the surface,
      glacier shrapnel once jagged, now tumbled round and smooth.
      Others, honey rivers wide and slow, the breeze
rich with warm clover.
   They made us light in their embrace, these rivers,
whether our bodies splayed them open
   or we lay beside them laughing in key with the timeless
rumble of water and stone; If I were a river
      I would be blue and brown and green at once;
         clear as glass, the stones bright, light, a rusty refraction.
      Would you swim in me again?
Would you ride the river inside me as you once did?
Could we both be born over in a rushing river of light and hope?
I wish I were a river.

from *The Puritan*
published in *Best Canadian Poetry 2016*

SUE GOYETTE ∞

On Losing Their Father

Eventually our grief, in the guise of a funeral home,

settled and we were offered the exhausted upholstery

of ritual. When we couldn't speak, we sat. The dreaded

silence was navigated by polished shoes and Kleenex boxes

reincarnated as kindling for the fire. Later, we will burn.

But for now we watched the framed print of *Flowers*

in a Vase narrate this wilderness. We knew, for example,

that our stems had been cut on an angle. That we'd been placed,

artfully, in a glass vase that reflects or rather infers the rest

of the room. One of us had dropped a petal and the rest of us

were flowering as hard as we could. Anyone with any heart at all

will feel for these chairs and the work they've got ahead of them.

*

The parking lot was the first indication. There was a series

of flower boxes in the insistent bloom of winter: the tulips of coffee cups,

bluebells of cigarette butts. What were we to make of any

of this? The taxi driver adjusted his small talk and what started off

as leashable and wagging ended up coming out of the woods quickly, furtively for a drink in his rear view mirror. He gulped in the red eyes

of our watches and their slow tick of too soon. He barely could take

our money. We barely could give it to him. It felt like he had come

to a full-stop at every tree, that he yielded to the Atlantic and signaled

before turning to the inevitable. We pressed our hands into his hands

and waited as if there was luggage to retrieve and a ferry to catch.

The laundromat across the street was open. We watched a woman

balance an impossible load and turned before she dropped anything.

There was only so much, at this point, we could give.

*

My children were like alders in the way they bolted

to tree. People stood at the roots of them and looked

up. They lined the hall to be in their shade. No one made room

for the small animals that had tangled their hair to scrabble

now, panicked by the walls. The carpets had been sprayed to resist

any kind of forest and here they were in full-leaf. Some people

wanted to touch them as if they were monks steeped in loss

and had tea to offer brewed from stories of broken bowls

and mountains to soothe them all. Some of them plucked their names

and carried them off to add to their evening meal of what they did

and who they saw. My daughter teetered first.

Later. When she was alone with the river that had been

her father. It was like she didn't mean it to happen,

that all she had wanted was to lean over

and drink.

*

I want to say that a tree fell, the way a tree falls and offers itself

across the water and when we encounter it, we don't see the fallen tree

but a way to get across. But she didn't fall across the water. She fell into

her father and I stood for many months at his shore and waited

for her. When evening came, I gathered wood and lit a fire.

I read the cursive line of ants and studied the emerald of bird song.

I ate mushrooms for the stews they'd make and drew maps

of the sky on the hind leg of moonlight. I picked river rushes and sewed

a small boat that could only carry the weight of my voice. In it, I packed all of her

names. Her secret names, her bedtime names. I stood at the back door

of her childhood and called to her with supper on my tongue. I bellowed

her bath time and urged her to run towards the net with the ball,

to give it a good and final kick. I sat up with her and spelled the difficult words

of farewell. Finally, I addressed her as woman. I combed the long hair

of her absence and sent fish scurrying with my feet.

*

She returned as a stranger and begged for a meal. I cut an onion

and heated the oil. When I offered her a plate, she had lost her appetite.

Often, she'd turn her head as if someone was approaching from a great

distance. She'd complain of the cold and then of the heat. Her treasure

was a small jar filled with her father's voice. She'd wake in the morning

with seaweed in her hair and a vague memory of low tide.

The distance between them was oceanic, she explained, which was why

she spent so much time at sea. She made films of herself wading into the ocean

and studied the angle of her heart to her arms. She choreographed her entry

into water to correspond with moonlight and the fine prow of memory.

When she heard a girl call for her father, she rescued the word

as if it had flown into a window. To see her crouch and pick it up,

soothe its eyes of terror and coax it back to flight. Once I saw her

open her treasured jar and quickly dab a paint brush into his voice.

All her portraits, when she was a girl, had their hands behind their backs.

She was no good at hands, she had explained, so she hid them.

*

I decided to follow her. Her hair has always been a lantern

and she cast an easy light. There is mining in my blood

which is why she chose me. I marked my trail with thorns

and seldom flowered. I stood far enough away that I couldn't hear her but saw the tender poise of her loss as she pleaded with an ocean

so sullen the waves broke silent. There is blood in my mining

which is why she chose me and so I rolled up the night and beat it

free of dark. I stood until I felt myself being tasted by the trees.

Eventually, they consumed me and in this way I could talk to him.

There was a marsh around our marriage that I sunk up to my knees in.

But none of him mattered and I had been consumed. My voice, when I pulled it

from the ground, sputtered the way root vegetables held to the light sputter,

freeing themselves finally of dirt. *Listen*, I said. When I could.

*

My leaves are uncertain and so I speak the truth. This is the ceremony

beginning. It isn't my voice that has his attention but my breath:

the little sparrow that flits past my heart and smells of home.

He is so young on this shore and has taken apart the only compass

he owned. His name is a flock fishing the shallow water, the wind

pushing it apart; the water, holding it under for too long.

He is surprised to see me. Surprised that I allow myself to be split

into boat. This is the work of marriage long after it has ended.

The paddle I push him off with is the vow I had once made.

*

A woman moves against the tide at the funeral home

while we're being offered strawberries and tea. She approaches us

as if we are without rock, our shore, sandy. Her name is Susan.

She speaks as if we are planetary, giving off such a light

that she is bathed in its blessing. She looks at my children

as if they are children. *I found your father*, she tells them. *I was the one*

who found him. Suddenly, they do not know what to do with strawberries.

Suddenly strawberries are something to be cared for, tended.

Nurtured. Should they sit down with the strawberries, they wonder.

Should they make a small bed for these berries and turn off the lights.

They are such small children to be making these decisions. They are such small

children that when she breathes the breath she has been holding for them,

they feel him with such force, they are blown close to sinking.

from *Room*
published in *Best Canadian Poetry 2014*

LAURIE D. GRAHAM ☙

Say Here, Here

Say cloverleaf, polyethylene. Say this parking lot
slinks into marshland, bristles into scrubland.
Say this mall becomes the world's biggest bonfire
and you travel its plastic smoke.

Say sky, fescue, say Wîsahkêcâhk,
say La Vérendrye and Henday,
say heart-choke, say groundbreak, say garrison
with gunbarrel eyes, say there's a fist
yelling this is my apartment now in a language
you don't know, say geno- matri- patricide,
say regicide, say terracide and skyocide,
say sapling, say childblood, cry doctor,
say your piece then get out, say translate, please
translate. Say coyote, say smallpox, say
creekbottom, look, Wîsahkêcâhk.

Say Big Bear.

Say Frog Lake, say fresh loam, say buffalo
hide, say free land, say thistle, aspen, sweat.
Riel, say Riel
can govern in Michif,

say colour, say colour-
less eye, say Queen's portrait, say here, here
is mine I bought it, say settler, claim
poverty, say better and see the felled trees,
say brethren, bread and wagons,
say Spanish flu, say railyard, sing
the combustion engine, say the singing
of your name in the new air, say virgin
territory and believe it, say the Lord's
bounty, say the wheatfields, say the dust,
pick the rocks, say canola and soybean,
thresh, thrush, say the laundry
on the line, say the dank root cellar,

say the numbers, tell the wheat board
where to go, say it fast like an auction and move

to the city, say minimum wage and grunt while you work,
say benefits, say rigpig derrick oilsand tailings pond boom,
say busted skull, say tuition fund and heritage fund, say concrete
scaffold, say it far from home, say the length of your commute
at the sound of the tone, say Ralph Klein and spit in the dirt.

Say Skydancer, say Zwicky, say
Alberta and Saskatchewan then
switch the order.

Say Wayne Gretzky Drive, say it's five-on-three
and he's on a break-away, scream it
in the riot on Canada Day, whisper it into your pilsner,
say it from the hollow of the couch, say it while you piss in the alley,
hiss it into your lover's ear,
say it to your broker and his secretaries, tell it to the lawyer,
to the landlord when the heat's shut off and the pipes freeze,
say it again to the food bank and again to the caseworker,

say cloverleaf highway polyethylene grocery sack.
Say fluorescent lightbulbs will save the earth, say there's a heart
in the middle of it (please tell me you can hear it),
say glut and democracy, say it in absentia,
say your little heartbeat, say it through the layers,
say it in the smoke of this blank, this bristling parking lot.

from *Room*
published in *Best Canadian Poetry 2012*

JASON GURIEL ❧

Spineless Sonnet

Your forearm supplies the sock puppet's spine,
your thoughts checker the sock's, your will argyles
the plain white weave. The sock's got half a mind—
though one half too few—to refuse to smile,
and grins and bears the voices in its head:
your four fingers and opposable thumb
miming the mouthful that cannot be said.
Elastic resolve slackens, lips once mum
now loose and sinking ships. But its windows
to the soul, salvaged from snowmen's sockets,
stay sewn on. De-boned, it sways when wind blows
like reversed Depression-era pockets,
and dreams of ventriloquist's knees, a pawn's
wooden posture, just one leg to stand on.

from *Maisonneuve*
published in *Best Canadian Poetry 2008*

PHIL HALL ☙

Fletched

A flower—no I mean one who—unplucked—flows / the *o* as in *holy*—not ouch

*

When I was 5—asleep on a fold-out couch—my cousin Clint Gordon 16
    sleeping there too

I woke up he was in me hurting me from behind I tried to get up he held me
    down *if you tell they'll send you to the bad place*

It probably happened to him the same way—about the same age—maybe even
    the same words

I wouldn't want to be literary here—but I wasn't awake in my life until then—
    not aware of myself as existing

My first *me* is this breach—a pain—the conviction that I am dirty—guilty

Words have their smells—they hit home

*

Try to think of the plucked stem as a crick—a creek—scared—in flood—lifted out

A three-leggéd meat-eating horse of a river—contorting—above lots &
    concessions

*

Cling to pathetic details: the Alcazar Hotel Vancouver Xmas 79 2nd floor corner

Contemplate foaming drizzle—down onto Pender—only a ballad mutters now

Stumbling those final tilted blocks into the bindle-stiff harbor—as if thrown / of
    hork & lard

My banjo's neck had cracked on the train—I threw a *Bic* as hard as I could against the wall & its plastic splintered

Later I crawled around—drinking from the bottle—hunting that pen's dark inner tube—*O mighty quill*—it wrote now—a pin-feather bendy to hold

No go the hotel / no go the song—or the cling-to—the long memory: gulls above slop near the Sea-View

*

Under what you can get away with—is the better line—what you can't get away from

Between sentimentalism—& misanthropy—is the worse mistake—writing to please

This fiddle-wind I tinker at squealing like goes: *Don't eat & read—come un-Protestant-ing*

*

I am always half / in love with the early / photos of at least / 3 women poets

Shame honed to defiant beauty—& often I am right: they have been abused also

Not only women—all of us who were made to—we were helpless—we absorbed fault

We who blinded half-truths—excoriated normalcy—told disgust a joke

To not end up in a ditch—to not go bonkers—to not become abusers—we had to tell

When we finally meet—we are safe dry old white flags—with these great eyes

Our lettered-halves long sunk deep into the red cork of the page

Our thumbed guide-feathers whistling

*

Not *holy*—better say *hardworn-sacred*

from *Forget Magazine*
published in *Best Canadian Poetry 2013*

STEVEN HEIGHTON ❧

Some Other Just Ones

a footnote to Borges

The printer who sets this page with skill, though he may not admire it.
Singers of solo expertise who defer and find harmonies instead.
Anyone whose skeleton is susceptible to music.
She who, having loved a book or record, instantly passes it on.
Whose heart lilts at a span of vacant highway, the fervent surge
    of acceleration, psalm of the tires.
Adults content to let children bury them in sand or leaves.
Those for whom sustaining hatred is a difficulty.
Surprised by tenderness on meeting, at a reunion, the persecutors
    of their youth.
Likely to forget debts owed them but never a debt they owe.
Apt to read Plutarch or Thich Nhat Hanh with the urgency of
    one reading the morning news.
Frightened ones who fight to keep fear from keeping them from life.
The barber who, no matter how long the line, will not rush the
    masterful shave or cut.
The small-scale makers of precious obscurios—pomegranate spoons,
    conductors' batons, harpsichord tuning hammers, War of
    1812 re-enactors' ramrods, hand-cranks for hurdy-gurdies.
The gradeschool that renewed the brownfields back of the A&P
    and made them ample miraculous May and June.
The streetgang that casts no comment as they thin out to let Bob
    the barking man squawk past them on the sidewalk.
The two African medical students in Belgrade, 1983, who seeing
    a traveller lost and broke took him in and fed him rice and
    beans cooked over a camp stove in their cubicle of a room
    and let him sleep there while one of them studied all night
    at the desk between the beds with the lamp slung low.
Those who sit on front porches, not in fenced privacy, in the
    erotic inaugural summer night steam.
Who redeem from neglect a gorgeous, long-orphaned word.
Who treat dogs with a sincere and comical diplomacy.

Attempt to craft a decent wine in a desperate climate.
Clip the chain of consequence by letting others have the last word.
Master the banjo.
Are operatically loud in love.
These people, without knowing it, are saving the world.

from *The Walrus*
published in *Best Canadian Poetry 2010*

JASON HEROUX ⚶

Allowance

After I finished my chores
I was given a raindrop
to spend in the woods,
I was given a shadow
to spend in the light.
A hook to spend
in the fish, a tank
to spend in the war,
a bird to spend
in the cage, a shiver
to spend in the wind.

from *Branch*
published in *Best Canadian Poetry 2016*

SEAN HOWARD ❧

shadowgraph 52: such a small splitting

(poetry detected in felix bloch's nobel physics lecture, 1952)

i

exodus—
light in the
desert

ii

'macroscale'—
time fielding
the moment

iii

war—
torn
stars

iv

man—
the loudspeaker
at the waves

v

alamogordo—
shades looking
at the sun

vi

'far away'—
crystal
night

vii

new verse—
'pure water/in a
natural field'

viii

'beyond recognition'—
the muse dead
in the fire

ix

the buddha's footsteps—
'cycles chained
to time'

x

ash—
split
light

from *The Fiddlehead*
published in *Best Canadian Poetry 2011*

HELEN HUMPHREYS ☙

Auden's House

The vice-Mayor meets us at the station
in a car meant for children's soccer—
bench seats arranged like pews in the back.
Each one a measured, isolated prayer.

The house is lived in now. Only two rooms
upstairs still marked as his. One the study,
and one the display. My ex-lover keeps
the vice-Mayor talking so I can sit

at the great man's desk, look down
into the garden where they had martinis
on the lawn. (He made a very stiff martini,
said the vice-Mayor, earlier.) The study

seems oddly Canadian, with its wood panelling;
cottage windows. A view to the green hills and the
sound of the highway. The chair is hard, straight-
backed. The desk smooth as paper under my hand.

Auden wrote every day. He loved writing, and this
is what I loved about him when I first started.
It seemed uncomplicated, his relationship to words.
But I was just young. I was uncomplicated.

"Poetry makes nothing happen," said Auden.
I could say it makes nothing good happen.
The choice is always the experience or the poem.
For a while you can pretend otherwise.

But it's really like this—an ex-lover
I've mostly ignored, keeps the vice-Mayor busy
so I can sit at the poet's desk.
Love is just the rough draft for the poem.

Isn't it? Or worse, the idea. The inspiration.
I don't want this to be the same, tired

story of youthful passion fading to middle-aged
apology. I don't want to write poems

with too many questions in them, or with the
bittersweet reflective moment as the geese fly overhead.
But it's already happened. It's always already
happened by the time you vow against it.

The geese don't care that they're a redemptive
symbol. At some point, shouldn't this matter?
"The body is the only truth," said Auden.
But, no, I don't believe that anymore either.

The body is the necessary truth. It's not
the only one.

I think this view is probably still your view,
Wystan. I like your neat rows of paperback
detective fiction. I like your ratty tartan
shopping bag behind glass, and the photo

of you stepping out of the grocery with it
over your arm, full of vegetables.

from *The Malahat Review*
published in *Best Canadian Poetry 2008*

MAUREEN HYNES ❧

The Last Cigarette

The last cigarette burned up all my creativity
and resolve: that was the risk.
I had to do my own hiding now. Straddling
a huge whitewashed log on the beach
past Massett, facing the tip of the peninsula
where Raven cracked open the clamshell
to find men hungering to get out (there
were no women yet): that's where I smoked it.
In sight of Alaska. Ocean, sky, rocks, pebbles,
smoke—I drew all those shades of grey
deep inside myself, held them in
and felt my smallest cells come to life and expand,
from my lips down into my web of bronchioles. I exhaled,
followed the spiralling smoke up to the clouds with my tongue.
I asked the Hecate Strait to wash
the longing out of me, to release me
from the consequences of that addiction.
Incinerate the desire
to an ash. Pluck it out of me, Eagle,
and trick me blind, Raven. To make
my sacrifice tangible, I left my white
Che Guevara lighter on the log. Plastic, faded, but
treasured. I slid off the log, walked in up to my shins
over the smooth-washed egg-shaped stones,
casting my craving everywhere, into tide pools,
beside the sea urchins and electric blue starfish,
under enormous boulder walls
and into the cold, cold surf.

from *The New Quarterly*
published in *Best Canadian Poetry 2010*

SALLY ITO ෪

Idle

in the pew as in life, awaiting deliverance from this dullness
that is all exhort and exhaust; where O Salvation art thou?
Sometimes it comes in fist-cherub face of the bawling infant's
cacophonous interruption, crow squawk to the sermon song,
insisting on milk and crumbs in the ever-present *Now*—
that is your idle alertness. Waiting, it seems, is a ponderous affair
and you have no time for it, this idleness that is the only state
that permits of dream, scheme, and imagine. And yet,
you are nonetheless here in the pew, attending the urge to
connect with world's soul weathers, its weal and woe
sometimes your own, you must admit. You are that car in park,
idling, engine humming, nowhere to go and that is as it should be,
you chastise yourself, squirming and ungrateful in your praise.

from *Prairie Fire*
published in *Best Canadian Poetry 2016*

AMANDA JERNIGAN ❧

Io

Your mother will not know you, your father
will not know you, your sister and your brother
will not know you, you will be driven
far away and you will live
in exile; then one day you'll be
permitted to return. And they,
as if you'd never been transformed,
will welcome you with open arms,
will call you by your given name.
And that's when you'll feel the change.

from *The New Quarterly*
published in *Best Canadian Poetry 2015*

MICHAEL JOHNSON ☙

The Church of Steel

Lathe, knurl, taper, thread: steel is god.
Oilsheened, bladeburnt by the kerf
of the tool's carbide tooth, see how
the excess molts, how the shavings rope
and wobble: the turned thing itself turned
bewitching. Shavings have scissored
my palms, worked straight through
my hands, made my skin a bloody bloom.
Yet I return to steel and emery cloth,
to lathed aluminum like razor lace,
to rust dust and drills and dies.
I play precision: hone, sink, buff, bore,
to see the coils sizzle and spin, knowing
my mastery is fleeting, and the cost—
these scars—simply offerings
to a god whose face I form.

from *Queen's Quarterly*
published in *Best Canadian Poetry 2009*

KHÂSHA ☙

Bush Indian

A young girl sat on the steps barefoot. It wasn't earthy, but poor and easy.
Beans was making his way to Honky Lisa's for a sip of goof.
And Violet was cutting up the moose meat that Joe brought over for her
It was a good day to die, or just watch…
The young girl was village
Cuddling a shyness that was given to her from her great-great grandmother
Whom she never met
A heirloom from her mother who died of pneumonia far far away
Beans could not die, could not live.
Just moving about as inconspicuous as an Indian drunk can be
He sat with Honky Lisa and sipped cheap wine by the window
I waved to him, and he waved back
Violet cut up that moose meat
Her knife was sharp too
It was like she wasn't even doing it, that's how easy it was for her.
I could see her at the kitchen table
She laid out a hunk of cardboard separating the moose meat that Joe brought
over
from the camp
Straight into the pot with some fat, carrots and potatoes
Me I just watch, cause today we're not born Indian, we grow into it
If I met Beans on one of his sober days, he'd say
Boy, you look like a whiteman, but you're making your way to be a good
Bush Indian
So I get busy because what the hell are words. I just shut my words up and
get the hell
busy.

from *Arc Poetry Magazine*
published in *Best Canadian Poetry 2014*

SONNET L'ABBÉ ☙

The Trees Have Loved Us All Along

That trunk there is alive. Up out of a paved patch in the concrete sidewalk at Main and Broadway and strung with blue lights in the middle of summer, that trunk there is alive. I'm in its space. It doesn't give me a hard time about it. Putting my smells into its air, lifting my arms or not lifting my arms there is always still the crook from where my limbs branch from my trunk, the crevices and what moss gathers there. Fragrances. That trunk there is smelling everything, tasting everything through its body. Leaves like tongues, salivating, tasting my cunt right through my cotton underwear, my cotton denim skinny jeans, my crevices all hot for him and only the fibres of plants between all our nakednesses, his and mine and the trees', whose love filled me up enough to be able to breathe it out through the porous bark of my defences. Hard on the outside, raw pith in here, that trunk hears all the plants in our local designers' industrial looms and in the aching polished skins of our flirty shoes, all the fibres and minerals making bodies of themselves and loving themselves and standing there rough and unremarkable and plain green-leaved between the parking meters, knowing us, knowing us so well.

from *PRISM international*
published in *Best Canadian Poetry 2010*

BEN LADOUCEUR ❧

I Am in Love With Your Brother

Richie made me promise not to relate any stories of
embarrassment or crime, but Richie, on
this, the evening of your nuptials, I must tell them about
our long day in Truro, I just must, the fallacy then
was a dark twin of tonight's fallacy, we
and the dogs—who are thought to be clairvoyant
on these matters—anticipated storms
that never came, and here we are now, beneath
a tarpaulin, on an evening they reported
would be clear and ideal for regattas.

As Truro woke, as birds of Truro wailed
morning song, Richie came across my notebook, open
to its core, where read these simple words:
I AM IN LOVE WITH YOUR BROTHER.
The first line, I insisted, of a song I'd been arranging
to be played on the Wurlitzer, though now I
come clean, Richie, while your soul is at its smoothest
and most forgiving, I did love him, the crimson acne
flecked across his neck, he was like a man
a guillotine had made an attempt at and failed.

We rolled that whole notebook into joints, didn't we
Richie, then drove into the boonies to shove ammo
into rifles folk left by their porch
doors. That summer, your brother's motorboat
slipped into the Irish Sea, his mannequin body
demolished, and I'll bet he is here now, and is
glad, I will bet, I am sure of this. Caroline, Richie
is one hell of a guy. You would do best to keep
his body firmly in yours, how seas contain boats, how
trees contain birds, for he is only stories to me now.

from *PRISM international*
published in *Best Canadian Poetry 2013*

FIONA TINWEI LAM ❧

Aquarium

Delicate, unworldly
seahorses behind the coral.
The grey one holds high
a noble, elaborate head.
The white one, belly full of young,
drifts near. Their tails entwine
as hands, even their unravelling
a slow caress. One hovers
while the other wanders
amid the anemones' waving tendrils.

Outside the glass,
my young son and I stand rapt
before this little paradise
as if it were a film
we must memorize
or perish.

His father has left us.
Probably for good.

from *The New Quarterly*
published in *Best Canadian Poetry 2010*

SANDRA LAMBERT ✂

Our Lady of Rue Ste Marie

Our lady of ste marie street
our lady of the cul de sac
our lady of chaste lawns
and roofs, intact

virgin of the stinking creek
virgin of the vacant lot

our lady of the airport
virgin of the smooth flight

Our lady of ville marie
our lady of the mountain and the river
madonna of mohawks
madonna of rapids
and massacres

madonna of *terra firma*
madonna of the new world

Our lady of quebec
metal virgin, incorporeal, hollow
our lady of granite
our lady of frost

our lady of incense
our lady of holy polluted waters
our lady of the mud and sludge of the river

pray for us

Our lady of fur
our lady of ice
our lady of live wires
our lady of sparks

immaculate virgin of snow

Our lady of pallisades and canons
madonna of missions and guns
virgin of smoke

our lady of traps
virgin of pelts, sinews and hides
virgin of knives
our lady of scalps
our lady of blood

virgin of voices
our lady of two tongues
and another one, forgotten

our lady of land claims
our lady of reservations
our lady of treaties, broken

Our lady of the recessed shrine and the domed ceiling
our lady of lilies
our lady of locks
our lady of ansoopial saints

our lady of the slender cross and the heavy hammer
our lady of stigmata
our lady of bones

Stained virgin made of glass
our lady of lead
our lady of the coin slot and the burning candle
virgin of the church and the casino

our lady of the gilt edge

Our lady of the organ and the sounding brass
tombless, wombless lady
of no relics

Virgin of amythest and silver
madonna of the muttered prayer
madonna of the thousand stairs
our lady of beads

Virgin of the black veil
virgin of the cassock and the swinging skirt

virgin of bells

Our lady of first communion
our lady of confession
our lady of depression

Nun of the thick tongue and the blunt fingers
virgin of wool

Our lady of sodomy by another name
our lady of love

Madonna of peregrinations
virgin of the v-formation
madonna of winter migration

our lady of geese

Our lady of the lake and the chemical toilet
virgin of duck blinds and screaming gulls
our lady of the great blue heron
our lady of the sharp-shinned hawk

our lady of owls

Our lady of beer
our lady of pepsi
our lady of ecstasy

Our lady of the swab and the syringe
our lady of the tampon and the pill

footless floating lady of weeds

our lady of *please, please, please*

Virgin of vegetation
virgin of genetic alteration
virgin of the potted geranium

virgin of tubers and bacteria and fungi
our unearthly lady of the decay of the body
virgin of worms

Virgin of polite parks and crude forests
virgin of bathtub shrines
virgin of bottled water
virgin of vinegar

our lady of e-coli

Our lady of white sails against the blue line of the horizon
our lady of fish and the turbid *fleuve*
our lady of star charts
our lady of mercury
our lady of floods

Our lady of antlers
virgin of trophy hunters

have mercy on us

Sweating lady of summer
lady of black flies, mosquitoes and bees
lady of blueberries and wasps
virgin of prickly heat

virgin of honey

Our lady of the screened porch
our lady of turnips and beets
madonna of the vine-ripened tomato

virgin of the waxy green bean

virgin of summer lightning

Invisible madonna of the blossoming orchards
our lady of apples
our lady of sugar
our lady of maples
our lady of butter and cream

our lady of the wooden spoon
and the pointing finger
madonna of the terrible mother

Madonna of marriage
our lady of domestic fights
our lady of incest
our lady of adultery
our lady of alimony
our lady of visiting rights

our lady of assault & battery
madonna of misogyny

our lady of love

Our lady of builders and masons
lover of carpenters
our lady of hammers and nails
patron of painters

Our lady of bills and loose change
our lady of the stock exchange
our lady of property

Virgin of appearances and disappearances
virgin of miraculous occurrences

our lady of refrigerators and trucks
our lady of billboards and toothpaste
our lady of road signs

our lady of the empty barn
and the looted grave

our lady of paradise, paved

Our lady of white linen and red wine
our lady of the chalice and silver plate

our lady of toxic waste

Our lady of wafers, soup kitchens and petitions
our lady of largesse
madonna of bandages and salves
our lady of hospital beds
our lady of SARS
our lady of chronic fatigue
our lady of ADD
virgin of the hysterectomy
our lady of AIDS

our lady of genital mutilation
our lady of infanticide
our lady of *suttee*
our lady of child
pornography

our lady of inoperable cancers
madonna of the mammogram
madonna of the MRI

our lady of the wire excision biopsy
our lady of the double mastectomy

virgin who runs for the cure

Our lady of artificial insemination
(our lady of the Annunciation)

Our lady of chaos, mutation, and change
virgin of asylum for the sane and insane

madonna of mad cow disease

Our lady of liberty & democracy
our lady of invasion of privacy
virgin of hostages
virgin of heresy
virgin of law
(our lady of lies)

virgin of politics
virgin of terrorists
virgin of electronic spies

virgin of holy suicides

Virgin of rape
virgin of genocide
madonna of the mass grave
mother of the child soldier
mother of the sex slave

Our lady of earthquakes
our lady of hurricanes
our lady of tidal waves

virgin of volcanoes

Our lady of logic
our lady of mathematics
our lady of nuclear physics

(virgin of x-rays
virgin of clouds)

Our lady of salvation
our lady of radiation
virgin of blistering skin

madonna of melanoma

Queen of the known universe
madonna of galaxies
our lady of black holes

madonna of the wobbly moon
(our lady of ozone)

Virgin of immaculate memory
(our lady of whitewash
our lady of history)

our lady of prophecy
our lady of gibberish
our lady of anguish

our lady of silence

Madonna of felicity
madonna of mystery
madonna of misery
madonna of mercy

madonna have mercy

madonna have mercy
madonna have mercy

on us

from *The New Quarterly*
published in *Best Canadian Poetry 2011*

M. TRAVIS LANE ☙

Bird Count

Kingfisher: dog collar, flash of light,
thread of invisible argument.

Coarse on the swaggering power lines,
an eagle's nest.

Larks mite-picking the sullen air:
thrust of tremendous business.

Grackles: a kind of croquet golf,
shove or be shoved.

A correspondence of pelicans:
a noon *Night Watch*.

An owl at night:
antennae of the frost.

from *The Malahat Review*
published in *Best Canadian Poetry 2013*

EVELYN LAU ◌

Grandmother

Today the news came: Grandmother was dead.
I rummaged through my body for a nub
of hurt, the way you might scour your teeth
with the tip of your tongue, searching
for the sore spot, the microscopic hole
in the dentine, the fracture along the gumline.
Found nothing. She hadn't spoken in years,
frozen and mute after a series of strokes—
this commander of twelve captives
whose favourite thing, my aunt admitted
with a sigh, was to yell.
She was famous for it, her voice a boombox
blasting songs of excoriation—
it echoed up and down the block
of that scorched California town,
boomeranging around the stucco houses
and cement gardens, a Chinese opera
of injustice and lamentation.
It would begin the moment she woke,
a growl behind the shut door
rumbling to a roar that ground on
until she brushed her teeth at night,
recriminations spat out
between mouthfuls of mint. My aunts,
her daughters, dominant in their own households,
wove around her like wraiths,
lips crimped, eyes downcast,
whispering in the wake of her wrath.
Wary of making a sound or gesture
that would set off the fusillade of blame.

Yet she never yelled at me, her first grandchild.
Praised the biscuits I baked in her kitchen
that summer I was ten, fluffy butter
and flaky pastry collapsing in her mouth.
It seemed I was on the proper path—
so clever I knew the phrases on Wheel of Fortune

before Vanna White could reveal another letter;
so reassuringly plain a cousin had to ask
if I was a girl or boy.
Grandmother still remembered the time,
as a toddler, I took care of her—
clutching her hand on the way to the store,
her bosom and stomach a warm bulwark,
her gold-toothed face beaming down at mine,
I had yelped and yanked her to a stop
just before she stepped into a mud puddle.
All day she praised me, as though I'd plucked her
from the precipice. Decades later,
wheelchair-bound, she flung out her good arm
to halt a great-grandchild from tumbling
off the kitchen table to the tile floor.

from *Ricepaper*
published in *Best Canadian Poetry 2011*

RACHEL LEBOWITZ ❧

from Cottonopolis

Tablecloth

In coffles they come, coughing, onto sloops, schooners, brigs, snows. On houses with wings! On snows! In Liverpool, snow falls on snows; in Manchester, it falls into the river Irk, onto chilblained Hands.

At the Castle, Governors Mould and Corps drink punch. The jungle encroaches. By next midwinter, the road will be gone again. And look at this cloth. White muslin, some fancy flower in the centre. A lily perhaps? What once were folds are now just holes, holes and holes. Below them, the table, stockings crawling with ants, the slave-hole. Above, a blue sky. Vultures on guns honeycombed with rust rise up to shriek their greetings. Hello, Hello. Here come the snows.

Jar

This is, after all, a new world. Iron brands, bands laid across the meadow, fallow field. They say cow's milk'll turn sour at the sound. They say the speed will crush your lungs. They say you could lie a sleeper line of mangled legs along this track. Wheels turn, the hare flees, rain falls in sheets. Over a hundred bales of cotton in her sides. We left Liverpool this morning. Some years back, there were signs in her windows. Silver Locks and Collars for Blacks and Dogs.

We'll reach Cottonopolis next. The train's greased with palm oil. See it shine.

Th gun goes off. Scramble!! Bodies shine. Slaves run, fling themselves overboard and are seized again. And later, we'll take this palm oil, this gold in a glass, and spread it on our trains and on our bread for tea.

Cask

Scow-bankers, beach horners, wharfingers: they haunt every port, brown-gummed and blind, spewing black blood. Bruises splotches of ink on grey paper. Gone the mouth, gone the legs, gone the sunburnt nose. Walk down this green road. I'll know thee by thine eyes.

The fog horn blows. Mersey Men unload barrels, shovel sugar, heave cotton bales. And in Bridgetown, Kingston, Roseau, sailors shiver and sweat. They huddle under derricks, hands curled over rotting toes. Crawl into this empty cask, sugar grit against the skin.

Everything is green here. Sweet sop trees, hibiscus for your true love's hair. The fog lifts. Heave away boys, heave away.

Muslin Dress

So here are lines of torn trees, dragged out by the roots. Lines of Redmen and squaws, curved line of babies on backs. Ragged line of footprints in snow.

Coffle line of Negroes, sent to clear land then fill it. Line of cotton in the field. Line of the lash. Twenty-five if the line of a leaf makes its way into the clouds of cotton. Twenty-five if the line of a branch is broken in the field.

There's that straight line the gun makes, the angle made with the torso when the arm is stretched out. The lines in the slave pen. The lines their fingers make as he moves them back and forth, to see if they'll pick cotton.

Here are the railway lines and there are the shipping lines. Here's the factory line. The line of children in the mines. The chimney lines. There is the line: from the cotton gin to the Indian.

The lines you've memorized, the lines of your white muslin dress, the way it falls in folds to the ground. All eyes are on you. For a moment, it's as if all lines stop here.

Photograph,   Negro

And ye shall know them by their fruits. They small lumps on his back, a bunch of grapes. Or this Negro's blackberry bramble! Raspberry, honeysuckle, rose. Head turned away. Hand on hip.

Crab-apples, dewberries, pine-apples, blackberries. Come by! Come by! The crops are in. Grapes shot—volleyed in the humid air. Ladies croquet, shuttlecock on silent lawns.

Do men gather grapes of thorns? Across the sea, bog cotton, purple heather, bees in clover. Upland cotton in airless rooms. Factory hands have arms and we have cut his off. We've made honey from the marrow of his bones.

from *Grain*
published in *Best Canadian Poetry 2012*

DENNIS LEE ❧

Slipaway

Of the metrophysics of ice:
slip away, seaboard.
In Greenland, a glacial divide—and
lost call for littoral cities,
slipaway Sydney.
London. Manhattan. Mumbai:
nostril meniscus, then ciao.
Or dykage, and stiltage, and humanoid critters
vying with dogfish for allsorts. Slip-
slipaway Athens, Rangoon, sub-
aqueous fables of *was*.
Rio. Vancouver. Shanghai—
slipslipaway Buenos Aires.

Cumuloss rising.   History slop in the wash.

from *Vallum*
published in *Best Canadian Poetry 2011*

SHELLEY A. LEEDAHL ❧

Single Pansy among Stones

Yellowest ear. Stepped on rather than around, and no sisters. Holy granite.
  Saladable? Perish that fancy.

Trying so hard to be the sun it hurts.

from *CV2*
published in *Best Canadian Poetry 2013*

KIRYA MARCHAND ❧

Hamlet

Houses by highways
Lunches by lamp,
Hamlet in highschools
hamlets and camps.

Hamlet the hero
Hamlet himselves,
Hamlet hermetic
high up on shelves.

Hamlet in Heorot
goldfish on hooks
Hamlet in whoredens,
hookers with books.

Hamlet in headphones
henhouses, huts,
Harvard and Hellmans'
hamsamwiches,

nuts. Historical
Hamnet, Hamlet
the Man. Heaven for
children, Hamlet

Japan. Horses for
Hamlet, Hamlet in
hooves, Yahoos for Ham-
let, Hot Cat Tin Roofs.

Why hello there Hamlet,
horrible friend,
Happy to see you,
how have you been?

"Hungry and harrow,
Hamburg to Hoth,

slings arrows vengeance
then am I off

"To houses by high-
ways, highschools and
homes, Lunches by lamp
light, Russia to

Rome." Oh Hooray, poor
Hamlet, homeless
and old. Prince of mankind,
Helvetica

bold.

from *The Antigonish Review*
published in *Best Canadian Poetry 2012*

DAVE MARGOSHES ☙

The Chicken Coop

The house my parents had built
for them went back to the bank
and we moved three miles down
the road to a chicken coop converted
to a crude home, and that's where I
learned first to crawl, then
to walk. Later, we moved deep
into an orchard of apples and pears
to an abandoned farmhouse
with a pond and snapping turtles
and eels. No chickens but geese
chasing the dogs with their eel necks
curved and it's here that I learned
to run, to talk, that I became the first part
of what I am. My father never overcame
his sadness at the loss of the house
he'd first drawn on a napkin at the Automat
on Lower Broadway—the house was gone
but he still had that napkin, crumpled
in the dresser drawer where he kept
folded money and his glasses. "It doesn't matter
how many new floors, how many coats
of paint," he would complain in his glass
of port, "you never get rid of the stink
of chickens." And he'd point
an uncertain finger at me. "Don't you
forget that. It's who you are."

from *Queen's Quarterly*
published in *Best Canadian Poetry 2010*

SADIE MCCARNEY ❧

Steeltown Songs

I.

All down the conveyor, the limes
bumped ends with a banged-up
mango and my checkout nerves.
Off work, soon. And then another

BOGO week, my lip gloss layered
on like sealant, a week of soap and fat
onion sacks hefted high to haggle
their worth. Nothing else to watch

but gas blots in a grimy overhang
of light, where a caravan of cabs
wear lit-up caps and idle more
smoke at smokers' backs.

II.

Sometimes the Axe-doused
after-school stock boys tackle
shelves with the force of a tag team,
sweaty and boastful in their show-off skill.

Brings it all back, though whether
it's them or just piss-warm coolant
from the on/off A/C, I couldn't say.
It's like ghost pains in a gangrened limb:

to spar with them! to flex with pumped-up steroid
pecs and vault them to the vertigo of ceiling tiles!
(all sense slashed by *4061-lettuce, 4041-plums,*
and an old recognition that dawns on me like drink).

III.

The new-bruised limes bump on past
checkout, and I stutter "cash-debit-credit",
then see. Spit-thin girl. A spastic 16,
nearer to bald and pitted by pockmarks,

who still watches worms ooze fatly in rain,
still skips a hopscotch to the chimes
on poor porches. Prue. Same grin—toothy,
lean of love—still half-stirring some

Cops and Robbers cool, half-known through
the soft swells of a roughed-up decade.
She is gaunt as sparerib in the
disaffected drought of June. Older, now.

IV.

Back then, me and Prue were coyotes.
Spooked mean and scrapping into fights,
we spat like it was our sole tiff with the mud-
plugged stone. Played tag, too, with the boys

(in roles, always Bad Guys or Mounties)
imagined other selves we'd rather be
jailed in a quarter hour twice daily. Back
in that cramped neighbourhood of knives,

Four Square was the thing each weekday:
a mangy tennis ball matted by dog drool
and hit over chalked-in lines. And dirt above all,
ingrained in denim, dusting a tanned crust of skin.

V.

Thursday Night Smackdown. These were
pay-per-view poets, gods of powdered cheese
and TV take-downs, and I knew war was a need
of skin. Broken bodies got tried on daily

like shin pads, mouth guards, never quite fitting
no matter how much their shapes got stretched
to *make* them fit. There were lives beyond lives,
sands beyond my little slit of beach and beer glass.

Wanted to earn belts myself someday. Or box,
The Meanest Bantamweight east of Toronto,
my triceps emboldened by barbells, blood,
and a bluish cancer courtesy of Maritime Steel.

VI.

Sometimes we skipped our chalked-in court,
our tire swing's welts of spit-out gum. Mondays
the dawn mist of strangers' pot did it—too much
bitter in the smell of sweet. Or too much sweet.

On those days we followed the ripped-up main road
like alley cats, strays mewing loudly for bones.
Past the dark, bloated bellies of trash bags brimming
with meat scraps, past chipped paint and chokeweed,

we wandered where train tracks scarred the town.
I dug for rail spikes loosed by boxcars while Prue
eyed the dank front of the building behind: self-storage
doors like little garages rusted shut and let lie for years.

VII.

Mildew, damp earth, plywood for windows,
a thin fire escape of warped gray boards.
Gang tags advertised the safety of standing,
so we left the earth and its spray-on bruises behind

to climb until ears popped and we saw in panorama.
The whole town: musty churches, the Liquor Commission,
and blue banks where the river swam its current
to trees. No rail, so we helped each other higher,

rocked like planes redirecting in air *higher*,
past gutters and patched-up doors. Busted boards
swayed below us like seesaws. Facing left: our North End,
the used mattress shop with just a bare spring on display.

VIII.

We saw it all: home, on Clover and Worth,
where the prefabs were mostly built of Insulbrick
and gin. Crushed-up cans in the mealy oaks.
There, we were one stock, whiteblackredbroke.

When the dizzy bloodrush of too much height
got Prue and we started to crawl back groundward,
we both thought past town lines we couldn't see.
And what might grow there. Dragged legs to Kwik-Way

where found change paid for half the counter:
nickel each for neon straws and grape-shaped gobs
dipped in sour sugar. Squinted hard and puckered
as we sucked. Like steeling for punches. Or for a kiss.

from *The Puritan*
published in *Best Canadian Poetry 2015*

DAVID MCGIMPSEY ♋

What was that poem?

My mother asked me, What was that poem?
It was Longfellow's "My Lost Youth," I think.
The answer was Longfellow, often enough,
even though she never liked Evangeline.

I talked to my mother on my cellphone
outside a grocery store in Philadelphia.
She asked me what I was buying, *Was it dear?*,
and if I now liked football more than baseball.

It was the last conversation I ever had with her.
I told her I liked baseball, to make her happy.
I knew she wasn't calling to talk sports.
She was showing off, saying, "I'm going to be okay!"

What was that poem? she'd say and act surprised
when I didn't know. It wasn't about the answer.
It was about noticing something held on to,
with wit and ferocity, until the day is done.

from *The Walrus*
published in *Best Canadian Poetry 2012*

DON MCKAY ☙

Sleeping with the River

All that winter as the rains arrived,
sometimes as nobody's footsteps,
sometimes as ack-ack, sometimes
hard bits of Braille flung at the house,
the mailbox, the woodshed, at the car parked
in the driveway, at all that is solid, all
that winter leaving the window open to its
pizzicati, hearing them accelerate and blend and
drown in the river's big
ambiguous chorus, all that winter being
swept asleep thinking river is only rain
that has its act together, song that has never
passed through speech, unschooled,
other-than-us, thinking
this must be the voice of what-is as it
seizes the theme, pours its empty opera,
pumps out its bass line of sea-suck and blues.

from *Brick*
published in *Best Canadian Poetry 2008*

JACOB MCARTHUR MOONEY ∞

The Fever Dreamer

(Baden Powell, 1918)

I have made the boys.
Baden boys, Britannia boys. I have made them cruel and handsome,
made them march in single file, backs straight, sleeping on their haunches
like new carnivores.

I have taught the boys
to take the waste from their lives, to cure their spit-cleaned trousers
of mange and leg and mittens. I've had my boys go post-European
and sew their pockets shut.

I have beaten boys.
I have whipped their face with eyebrows. I have singed their shirts with steam
and broken out the laxatives. I have proctored international, made
and been remade by boy.

I have told the boys
I Want Them. I want them for king and kaiser. Want them Lusitania
and Sino-Tsarist tensions. Want them cradle of statecraft
and Metternichs and mobs,

want armament contracts
for agreed-upon fathers, mothers who would pack-mule pamphlets
into bedrooms, the boyish Yes! of Oxford Press, printing (in three
weeks) *Why We Are At War.*

I have become the boys'
sincerity, their sweated-out details. I have boxed the boys,
bent them at their waists and wound their backs for marching.
If you scratch my surface,

I will be the boys' defense.
I'll settle their wounds with the Good News of Field Dress. I will
wear them hats. I will tie them heads to handkerchiefs. You'll taste how
I have egged them on,

how I've fed the boys
provisions. In those first provocations of union hall or field,
I've shown them the fruitful economy of hunters, bought them
the blades for first shaves.

With the saccharine blood
of their comeuppance, I have calmed them. I've shown them to suckle on
the nearest teat to tongue. I have left them to tend to these friendships
in dark habitats.

The boys, as boys, descend
on repertoires of bravery. I know I bring it up again,
but look at what they're wearing. Observe the benevolent
cotton at their necklines,

their badges and banners
torqued into hieroglyph: Boy at swim. Boy at camp. Boy against
the outline of the nation that protects him. Boy using arrow.
Boys embraced around a flame.

I apologize
to Europe for the invention of the boy. I did not design them
to be tyrants or marauders. I didn't dream them up to die.
I demanded of boys

that they drift in mythic
packs, wicked on the scent of antagonist or sibling. I regret
that climactic lifting of the fence, the appeal to factor in
the fattened hearts of kings.

I have brokered boys,
bankrolled their littleness and lust. I've erected border towns
both between and inside them, built hives in their minds,
free from history.

Cornered in this keyhole
nightmare of Brittany, I've engendered all the boys, as brood
and as bereavement. Call me piper, boogeyman, but it is true
I made the boys.
I have made the boys bewildering.

from *Arc Poetry Magazine*
published in *Best Canadian Poetry 2013*

CARA-LYN MORGAN ❧

mîscacakânis

Watrous, 2012

you are my yearling. I have brought you here
to give to you the prairie, a place to be human

and small and at mercy. In the evenings, you sleep
and I breathe a scatter of Michif into the soles

of your feet. You are mîscacakânis
my little coyote, running along the scattered flatland

with your arms above your head. Screaming, casting
your long shadow out on the narrow railway line.

We taught you to swim in Lake Manitou, the weightless
surf, then washed the salt from our skin

in the outdoor shower. In the morning
I braided sweetgrass in your hair and then you ran

barefoot and unafraid, shaking the dew
from yellow canola. You drift off in the afternoon

smelling of soil and sweat, sunlight and crop.
I have brought you here

to give to you the only thing
there is. May you be wild here,

a girl-pup, mine
from long ago.

from *Room*
published in *Best Canadian Poetry 2015*

A.F. MORITZ ❧

The Clock

The clock began to tick. Or I began
to hear it in the room where it had always
ticked and I had rested. The rhythm

appeared, like blood that had been there
circling invisible that surges from some cut,
that bursts open a flaw. A spurt, another,

regular. Won't they ever end? Won't it run out?
And it keeps running out, the blood in the terrified
attention fastened on the fountain. The drops

fall on the floor, gather, and flow out of sight
to harden somewhere, lose the nature of blood,
be knowable as blood to the scientist only

who comes later, tests the dust
and says at the end of scrutiny, This is blood.
The motionless face of the clock had begun

to forge forward, in that room that long had held
my body lying still. It was speaking now
a rhythm that ought to underlie a song. A rhythm

made by the mind's arithmetic, as it figured ways
the skein of featureless ticks could be arranged:
iamb and trochee, spondee, dactyl, amphimacer,

all the paeans... A rhythm that made my breath stop
with conviction the next tick wasn't coming. Star systems
were conceived and died in the silences

between each two. "Unbearable suspense," it's called:
the heart expecting to recognize it's dead,
it's been dead while the brain had to wait

a further second—the length of all true thoughts—
for the blood's stoppage to reach it. Impossible, that ticking.
It can't exist. In my room, in the resting of my body

there was no time, no future for any new sound
to come from or to sound in. All was silence.
And yet the ticking had come. So all was now

a prow moving in a sea
of black places that were not
till it cut into them. The voice of the clock

went on that way in my craw, dragging me
between excitement and exhaustion
while I longed to be left alone, to be restored

to the quiet of before, where I was paused
permanently, to consider until I could grasp it
this being underway.

from *NewPoetry*
published in *Best Canadian Poetry 2016*

SHANE NEILSON ∞

My daughter imitates A.Y. Jackson's "Road to Baie St. Paul"

> *But that free servitude still can pierce our hearts.*
> *Our life is changed; their coming our beginning.*
> —Edwin Muir

The life locked in pastoral: ramshackle barns the colour of varnish,
burnt roofs, fences that raise arms from their sides until their arms
fall exhausted upon the earth. The fences are angels and the farmhouses
containers for men and women who know the fields with nothing
but the horse and the plough.   O send me your angels
now, I will fix them with the bit and set them to work upon the scene:
to make angel-forms in the snow. The mountains slumping in the
     background
are for farmers and wives to set lives against, to wonder how many days
it would take to climb the slope, if they would turn back and see their homes
imprinted in the snow of the fields, if they would turn to salt by turning
     around,
the salt cracking down the mountainside, the salt a true snow.
Then the work starts again and the trees for colour stand in place as guards.

The beautiful polices the most solemn passions. The only man who can be
     seen
is in the cold, coming home or clearing a path with his horse ahead.
My daughter built this place with its limited range, let the structures collapse
and lean, the ache of unseen men and women held in their places and
     homes,
not a brushstroke that identifies the Canadian Shield, her ancestry, or the
     man in view.
Who could it be, and where is this, and why? I think I've lived there all my
     life,
with no little girl to see, feeling the angels condescend to the scene
as guardians of the spare. *Take heart*, I tell the man, and *Hurry*.
Find them, make sure they are inside.

from *The Fiddlehead*
published in *Best Canadian Poetry 2015*

HOA NGUYEN ❧

A Thousand Times You Lose Your Treasure

She mistook the munitions for fireworks

She said goodbye to her lover

She threw the photographs in the pond

She dressed as an 'old woman'

She shaved my head (my hair too light from the white father)

She took off her jewellery

She took in neighbours   but not by choice

She could have been labelled 'a counterrevolutionary'
           and dumped into a mass grave

She would have said that I wasn't her baby

Tet 1968

from *Event*
published in *Best Canadian Poetry 2015*

DAVID O'MEARA ♋

Background Noise

Home, my coat just off, the back room
murky and still, like the side altar of a church, so at first

I don't know what I hear:
one low, sustained, electronic note

keening seamlessly across my ear. I spot
the glow of the stereo, left on all morning,

the CD arrested since its final track, just empty signal now,
an electro-magnetic aria of frequency backed

by the wall clock's whirr, the dryer snoring in the basement,
wind, a lawnmower, the rev and hum of rush hour

returning on the parkway. I hit the panel's power button,
pull the plug on clock and fridge, throw some switches,

trip a breaker, position fluorescent cones to stop the traffic.
But still that singing at the edge of things.

I cut down overhead power lines, bleed the radiator dry,
lower flags, strangle the cat

so nothing buzzes, knocks, snaps or cries.
Then I shut the factories, ban

mass gatherings, building projects and road work,
any hobbies that require scissors, shears, knitting needles, cheers,

chopping blocks, drums, or power saws. It's not enough.
I staple streets with rows of egg cartons. I close

the airports, protest the use of wind farms, lobby
for cotton wool to be installed on every coast. No luck.

I build a six-metre wide horn-shaped antenna, climb
the gantry to the control tower, and listen in.

I pick up eras of news reports, Motown, Vera Lynn, Hockey
Night in Canada, so attempt to eliminate all interference,

pulsing heat or cooing pigeons, and there it is:
that bass, uniform, residual hum from all directions,

no single radio source but what I'm told is resonance
left over from the beginning of the universe. Does it mean

I'm getting closer or further away? It helps to know
what bounds there are, whether we're particle, wave or string,

if time and distance expand or circle, which is why
I need to learn to listen, even while I'm listening.

from *Quarc* (a joint issue of *Arc Poetry Magazine* and *The New Quarterly*)
published in *Best Canadian Poetry 2012*

MICHAEL ONDAATJE ☙

Bruise

In the medieval darkness of the Holland Tunnel
with luminous green paint, on whitewashed walls
of the Madrid zoo, in his thick-fingered handwriting
onto dust at the dry Casablanca aquarium

> *"When last I held you in my arms,*
> *my love, the West African Black*
> *Rhinoceros was still magnificent*
> *and still alive…"*

What have you been doing to Paul Vermeersch?
He has searched for you encyclopedically
in Albacete, in Zagora, in those cities
whose names have changed,
till the maps he relies on wear out.
In what disguise did you leave him?
So he will not recognize
your gait anymore,
or your stare out from a diorama.

Hunt and Torment. Call but no Response.
In the end words of love reveal
just yourself. Not why
or the wished-for thing. Only the Spanish
consider his plea, only the drivers
deep in a tunnel into New York
nod wisely, agree with him.
But it is the black rhino whose loss they mourn,
not the person he held once in his arms.

When it is over, it is over,
they say in the passing dark.
There are no longer great nostrils
to scent out the source of torment.
It is a generation since our love,
to justify anger, had a horn, a tusk.

from *The New Yorker*
published in *Best Canadian Poetry 2014*

P.K. PAGE ⟨ℬ

from Coal and Roses: A Triple Glosa

3

> And the miraculous comes so close
> to the ruined, dirty house—
> something not known to anyone at all
> but wild in our breast for centuries.
>
> —*Everything is Plundered...*
> Anna Akhmatova Tr. Stanley Kunitz and Max Hayward

There is a place, not here, not there. No dream
nor opiate can conjure it—it is
not heaven, though heavenly—it is its own
element—not sea, not earth, not air,
nothing approximate, nor half way matched,
where other laws prevail. It honours those
who enter it like water, without wish
vainglorious or trivial—a gift
from realms of outer unimagined space.
And the miraculous comes so close

it alters us. It is as if a beam
embraced us and transformed our molecules
and merged us with some cosmological
and fractal universe we never dreamed,
more vast than any thought we had of love
divine or secular, a synthesis
of right and wrong, of midday, midnight, dawn,
of poverty and wealth, sackcloth and silk.
A gift of coal and roses
to the ruined, dirty houses

and to their opposites—the shining palaces
floating above in towers of cumulus—
that take on size the way a child's balloon
can fill with breath, or perfume scent a room.
This beam—not tenuous nor crystalline,

minus proportions, neither large nor small—
is all encompassing, a kind of womb
a "heaven-haven" and improbable,
some entity beyond recall.
Something not known to anyone at all.

And yet it is our heartbeat, intimate
and human. Here, my wrist—its pulse
is yours for the taking, yet it is not yours.
We share a heartbeat, share lub-dub, lub-dub.
All races, genders, share that little drum
and share its Drummer and its mysteries.
This quiet clock, unnoticed day by day,
our ghost attendant, is invisible,
untouchable, perhaps sublunary,
but wild in our breast for centuries.

from *Descant*
published in *Best Canadian Poetry 2009*

ELISE PARTRIDGE ⚬℥

Two Cowboys

He yanked the child along,
six years old? dressed like him—
ebony snakeskin boots
scuttling through blaring cabs;
black bolos fluttering;
hats bobbing, black rolled brims.

Were they running late for a wake?
The father scowled. His nose
was gnarled, a boxer's;
blond ponytail fraying, slicked.
The boy tried to keep pace—
skittered along on scuffed toes,

lurched off a curb. The man
swore, quickening his stride.
Oh not to be left behind
when all you clutch is one hand!
Was the boy saddlebag freight
flung on for aching rides?

At the light, he glanced towards me.
Brown colt-eyes, wary, full.
Let him be dashing from shifts
at the fair's Wild West tent.
Let me not find him years on
tossed, by broken bulls.

from *The Walrus*
published in *Best Canadian Poetry 2009*

RUTH ROACH PIERSON ☙

Equipoise

Over a shared lunch, our first
in two years, Valerie announces
she's reached a stage in her life
when she just wants

to float—not like a kite
or a helium balloon loosed
from a child's grasp, but *float*
as her mother, eight months pregnant

with a younger sibling, shouted
from the shore the time Valerie
waded into water too deep
for her six years. Hearing the fear

in her mother's voice, she
relaxed into a float, face-up,
mouth out of water and thus
survived.

But to stay afloat, I muse, requires
treading water, an activity I find,
at this stage in my life, too
similar, in Seattle parlance,

to dinking around. So instead
I rush backwards and forwards
between irreconcilable sets
of imperatives, awe-struck

by the iron serenity I observe
in the hawk circling overhead, borne
aloft on air currents yet able,
at a moment's sighting, to drop

into a swift dive. Aim spot on.

from *Grain*
published in *Best Canadian Poetry 2013*

MEDRIE PURDHAM ❧

How the Starling Came to America: a glosa for P.K. Page

> *Their eyes flash me such mysteries*
> *that I am famished, am ill-clad.*
> *Dressed in the rags of my party clothes*
> *I gather their hairs for a little suit.*
> —P.K. Page, "Invisible Presences Fill The Air"

It was that teen who made our sky inscribable.
Juliet. *I would I were thy bird*, she said. The tickle
of her eyelashes made everything salient. Her lover,
needing more time, called the lark the owl. Made day
night. Even the sun pulled back into its harbour.
But as the world dawned behind the cypress trees,
the mud was credible and the air was chill.
Look, who wouldn't go as far as that girl's lover?
Someone thought to make the New World up of these:
      (*their eyes flash me such mysteries*)

one of every bird mentioned by Shakespeare. Someone knew:
everyone wants providence in the fall of a sparrow,
and wants their pretty chickens not to die.
Everyone wants (whatever they say) some kind of
garrulous, even some kind of authored,
made-articulate sky. Dear America: here's a fad,
here's the starling. One of the bard's. It speaks
nothing but "Mortimer," so Shakespeare says. Well, but
I remember Shakespeare's nature. In it, Lear went mad.
And *I* myself *am famished and ill-clad.*

No, nothing but "Mortimer," and even then,
Death claimed the first syllable, claimed it anyway,
could still abrade the word. Could scoop its sense:
could get there first. Could fail to recompense
literature for its gesture. That's what the starling says
in idiomatic starling. So I compose
these lines while sitting by the window, hoping
inside and outside will coalesce.

I have a Grecian urn and a Roman nose
and am *dressed in the rags of my party clothes.*

I have a pan flute too, the better to entrance
my johnny-come-lately aviary. *I would I were*
thy bird, she said. A star-crossed girl.
The leaves the starling parted were a book's.
The world through which I wend my way is made.
I stroke the animals of which the poets wrote,
I siphon from their shadows; I call them
introduced. Mine is the New World; all I've known.
I stuff the birds (*thy bird*) and pluck the fruit,
I gather their hairs for a little suit.

from *CV2*
published in *Best Canadian Poetry 2014*

BRENT RAYCROFT ❧

S and X

The S not the X is sexy in "sex."
Sure, X is the crux, it's the hardcore act,
crotch into crotch, little swords crossed. But S!
S is the motion: push forward, push back.

Happy they're both in the same little word.
One so angular, the other so curved.
And in between them the wise letter E
suggests with a gesture "You two should meet!"

X is the end point, the strong closing kiss.
S is the start, the fold in the robe
as gravity takes it, the audible hiss
of the breath as we improvise poses.

S is the yes that could still be a no,
so that X once again may stand for unknown.

from *FreeFall*
published in *Best Canadian Poetry 2014*

SHANE RHODES ❧

You Are Here

Though not endorsed by the treaty commissioner, I would like to
acknowledge this book was written in the said country
While this book was written, contested territory was tested
I would like to acknowledge the Secwepemc, the Cree and the
Algonquin nations, upon whose territories this book was written
                    The land was "shovel ready"
I would like to acknowledge I did not ask for permission, that I
felt too uncomfortable to ask and didn't know how to, that I don't
know if asking is the answer because I barely know the questions
I would, however, like my acknowledgement to be acknowledged
Warning: this book is not about faraway lands, Greek and Roman
philosophers, Japanese haiku masters, and Elizabethan poets will
not be discussed
                    This book is about desire
            the desire to look elsewhere
This book is about where I live, a place still settling, still making
the land—law by law, arrest by arrest, jail by jail—its own
                    snow blown
As stipulated in subparagraph 12(1)(a)(iv), paragraph 12(1)(b) or
subsection 12(2) or under subparagraph 12(1)(a)(iii) pursuant to
an order made under subsection 109(2), a dispute cannot be made
under this section of my book
Warning: this book of verse demands more of verse, this book
demands perversity
This book uses words as heard in annual reports and business prospectus,
the smooth cadence of policy platforms and parliamentary
committees, the shouts of protesters and riot police
This book, also known as *The Heart of Whiteness*, terries in Indian
territory, my terra firma, where all intercourse is, of course, governed
by the official *Indian Intercourse Act*
Making land: here is a YouTube loop of me stepping from my
Legend 12' Ultralite aluminum boat with its Mercury 2.5-HP fourstroke
engine, book in hand, claiming all this as my new found land
This book, also entitled *What??*, is part of my much larger Amnesia
Project, created with generous support from the Ministry for
Elective Memory

This book is new—groundbreaking people moving tree clearing
root pulling concrete pouring factory building new
Tired of maintaining the holes in its language, tired of staying
silent, so tired of forgetting, this book
This book, marking its territory on virgin snow and barking at the
fenceline, is about the settlers' dream of legitimacy
Warning: the reading of this book while at a game between the
Eskimos, Blackhawks, Braves or Indians, sponsored by Mohawk
Gas, within a vat of melted Land o Lakes sweet cream salted butter,
chewing Red Man tobacco, while listening to "Indian Giver"
by the Ramones, may be dangerous to your health
This book was written in the gaps between words written and
words spoken, words meant and words meant only to fill the space
of meaning
This book I will continue to write until I get it right, and I will
never get it right
About a land held by therefores, herebys and hereinafters, this book
        la terre de ma mère
This terrible book, with its inter-racial terroir, was written on an
interrogated territory of error
Warning: reading this book could be harmful. See this picture of
Jim, he has cancer and says "I wish I'd never started reading"

from *The Toronto Quarterly*
published in *Best Canadian Poetry 2014*

ELIZABETH ROSS ☙

Mastiff

for Milton

i.

The dog is sick, seizures.
But still he guards our kitchen window,
eyes two dark pits
of expectation.
                I have to approach
the front door carefully, too much excitement
and he stiffens as if struck, folds, a slow motion
metallurgical wreck, two hundred and twenty resonating pounds
quiver on the floor.

He thuds his tail against the wall
before enclosing me

in a pounding circle, floor quaking,
tipped-over salt and pepper shakers on the table
rolling concentric rings.

ii.

Walking him is like walking night
into sun. Brindle at the end

of a braided leash, his rusted scent rising.
Commuters slow to a crawl, mouths unfurl.

He keeps close to me,
never pulls, our waists level

as we lever paw, shoe, paw
in time down the street. Two thousand years ago

he fought lions in coliseums. Now I watch him stalk
a hollow ball filled with peanut butter

in the living room and wonder about the taste
of blood. He shakes his head,

flings a joyous stretch of drool
as tall as a man above him.

iii.

The problem is his heart.
His veterinarian says the next step will be a dog
cardiologist, then a pacemaker
harvested from a cadaver—a human mechanism keeping

time for him. To prevent further trauma,
beta blockers prescribed.

I loosen his collar, thumb a fleshy pill
into a wedge of cheese and jam.
For a belly rub, he pours himself
onto his back, memory
intractable.

iv.

Electricity uncages in his chest, arcs

                        through the septum-hole, conducts itself

across each rib-bridge to the conduit

            of spine, sparks each limb rigid, ruffs a static

topline. The humming

        rings him in, vision ore-marbled, enclosed

by an aureole sky. He's been here before, deafened,

iron-tongued. The weight

of predator eyes. His skull sockets

fear-rush, blind.

v.

With each attack, I'm supposed to leave him
to battle on his own, eyes swiveling, piss
arching through the air, back snapping
his limbs into acceleration.

The vet has warned. One day he'll wake
up the way he normally does
but won't recognize me, will try to kill
the first animal he sees.

To keep a dog like this
alive: is it fair
game because we love each other?

I wipe the foam from his lips,
hold his shoulders,
my head in the lion's mouth.

from *Prairie Fire*
published in *Best Canadian Poetry 2013*

LENORE & BETH ROWNTREE ☙

7 lbs. 6 oz.

Some things about my sister Beth
that I can't think about for too long
without getting sad and confused:

1. The time we went to the Bracebridge
Dairy for cherry pie and vanilla ice
cream and she took too long in the
bathroom, so I kept knocking on the
door, and when she emerged she said,
"My life is hard, you know."

2. The time I blew snot out my nose
and rubbed it in her hair in front of
the boys from down the way who
were already afraid of her.

3. The time my cousin said at the family
reunion that she ruined everything.

4. The time some kids threw snowballs
at us on the way home from school,
and the ones they threw at her had
stones in them.

5. The time a man gave her an engage-
ment ring that was too big for her
finger so it came off during the night
in her bed, and the staff at the group
home found and returned it to the
man, who'd spent his disability
allowance on it, and she thought he
had broken up with her because she
lost the ring, and nobody ever told
her anything different.

6. The time I looked in her purse and
found nothing but scraps of paper so
covered in writing there was hardly
any white left on the pages.

7. The time my mother told me she had
a normal birth weight, 7lbs. 6 oz.,
but an abnormal delivery because a
bully nurse shoved her back in and
held her until the doctor arrived.

8. The first time she became an
outpatient at the Clarke Institute of
Psychiatry and wrote this list to
remember the layout:

11th floor
Dr. Jeffries' Office
9th floor
8th floor
7th floor
6th floor
5th floor
4th floor
3rd floor
Day Care Centre
Ground Floor
Chapel

9. The time I found her poem "Lies" in
her wastebasket:

Happy
Jolly
Jovial
Pretty
Funny
Beautiful
Cheerful, Pleasant
Lovely, Sense of Humour
Educated, Famous, Smiling
Lies, Full of Lies, A Wheat Sheaf
    Full of Lies.

from Geist
published in *Best Canadian Poetry 2010*

ARMAND GARNET RUFFO ℭ𝔰

The Tap is Dripping Memory

My mind is a town with Main Street looking
like it's had its teeth punched in.
Its eyes blackened. Broken windows and empty lots.
And, then, it's a bright Saturday morning, and
I'm riding my bike down to the beach.

My parents relax on creaky lawn chairs.
I can hear their every move. They are in the shade
of a house made of bone and tar paper.

My sister is screaming the house is on fire. We run
to the Japanese neighbours. Exiles like us, my mother whispers.
In their tiny kitchen, we drink cocoa where everybody is safe.

My aunt is in a western bar dancing. She throws her cowboy hat
in the air, revealing her bald head.
Everyone turns away except me.
Then my sister says she doesn't want to die,
but she dies anyway.

I am ten again. We go for a family picnic, and I get car sick.
The dust from the road in my hair, clothes, mouth.
When we arrive I jump into a lake,
and find I can't swim. My father drags me out.

When we return a neighbour is skinning a bear on his back porch,
as if it's something he does regularly.
The bear is staring at me. His eyes get bigger and bigger,
until they become moons.

I arrive at a friend's door just in time to overhear him
say I swear and don't believe in sin. His parents
tell him I'm just a little pagan.
I creep away trying not to be noticed, but the floorboards
thunder with every footstep.

At home my dog Chopper is smiling at me with a curled lip,
and I am loving him in a moment so perfect the world opens for me.
The moment is a silver hook cast into a bottomless lake.
Floating until it sinks.

It's true. Some memories cannot be turned off with sleep.
I jolt awake, go for a glass of water, pull the curtains aside.
The light in the yard beside the tree is hard yellow.
The dripping tap punctuates the night.

from *Event*
published in *Best Canadian Poetry 2010*

JOY RUSSELL ☙

On King George's Crowning

On King George's crowning, the interviewee
said they all got sweets and little goodies, and when
they come by boat, some come as stowaways. Once

they collect money for this woman's fare. Others
come, a fiver tight in their pockets, like my grandfather
when he escaped from the belly of the crown and never

spoke of it again. Others not bring overcoat—
no one told them how air moves vampires through
bone, erases memory matter. Some dress in suits

tropical style, as the ship moved its shaky
hand over the old surface of the sea. They arrive,
say 'I born Jamaican, I die Jamaican,' take a bite

of the sweet, hand to mouth, take the test
of motherland's history—bitter—replied, when asked if
they spoke the Queen's English; Enoch Powell's rivers

of blood forming a new oxygen, scarlet-marked
as they sliced through London fog; iris recording
life, how it is: Houses of Parliament, Big Ben

in the grey dank; a room, a galvanized tub to wash, emerge
baptized; the city soot, a new glove for the body; the signs
reading no Irish or blacks or dogs, not wanted but

take your money, just the same. Some, some,
carry hope like luggage, others not so sure-footed, others
not so childlike in believing all what this mother have to say.

Some bring formal names, leave pet ones behind,
whisper night bougainvillaea. How this country
cold, cold, cold through and through and no tea hot

enough to warm you, or hand friendly enough to pry
open the dark days, bring morning brightness. Some come,
stay, patience worn thin like paper, hearts

tough as old bread, and letters back home with every
copper earned from the Double Decker, brow wipe
of the sick, hammer of nail into two by four—if they

let you, if you not too dark for their liking.
Some, some, come long way, did bite
of the sweet. Motherless mother's milk.

Ol' Englan'
cryin' crocodile tear
for her lost chil'ren.

from *The Capilano Review*
published in *Best Canadian Poetry 2008*

ROBYN SARAH ❧

Messenger

Little stone in my shoe,
what have you to tell me?
That such a tiny irritant can serve
to undermine a meditative mood
hard-won from day's commotion
by a walker on the mountain?
That I am obstinate, who will not stoop,
or stop to teeter on one leg
and tug at sandal-straps—
prefer to hope you'll work your way
out, same way you sidled in,
without my intervention?

Are you a stowaway—fugitive,
or just adventurer
hopping a ride to town,
a roadside pebble with big-city dreams?
Are you a terrorist—dispatched
to tell the plight of kindred
tired of being trodden on?
Are you a grain of sand,
seed for a pearl to my oyster brain?
Are you an augurer?

You cling and dig in
even to toughened skin,
and will not be appeased.
Little stone in my shoe,
what makes me choose
to walk with you awhile?
What little creeping guilt
accepts it as my lot
that you should harry my sole
the whole way home?

from *The Fiddlehead*
published in *Best Canadian Poetry 2010*

BRENDA SCHMIDT ☙

A Citizen Scientist's Life Cycle

In summer the culvert didn't seem so mean, just dried up like everything else.

1.
Pulsing darkness. A chorus without pause
issues forth from the culvert's mouth
as it does throughout the year, spring flows
peaking now, beating me and the metal both.
A bit dramatic perhaps, but that's me
these days, feeling my age, my crooked toes
digging at my boots like gophers fleeing
too late the strychnine found in their burrows.
The colourless and bitter can make life
one long convulsion, a violent rush
from end to end. I hear the half-
crack of my knee, wonder who in the bush
will note the trudge, the hunch, conduct yet
another survey. Just me, I bet.

2.
Another survey. Just me, I bet,
here in the ditch, listening for owls.
I set the timer for two minutes, forget
tick by tick as timed minds do when strict rules
demand stillness. Hearing the click of crowns
in the wind brings shivers. Black spruce are evil
queens in this light, or Baskerville's hounds
gnawing the wet hollow in which I dwell.
The alarm sounds. Then a long staccato
from the east, as if blood-crazed gundogs
are cheering the hounds on. God only knows
why an owl sounds like this, or why my legs
nearly buckle on impact, like a deer
gut-shot, heading for cover, the bluff near.

3.

Gut-shot, heading for cover, the bluff near:
life is a passage and here I am, prey
preying on fear. A hunter always fears
the animal inside that waits for the day
it reveals itself. A spring bear, hungry,
slow-hearted, ambles toward the bacon
grease and fish guts, chocolate cookies,
the spot I fail to scrub off my hands.
Standing here, I am bait. The smell lingers.
I am drawn to it as usual.
Down the road, I'm told, a trail cam captures
passing deer, the odd coyote, vultures, all
in black-and-white, like any memory.
I squatted there last week. Too much coffee.

4.

I squatted there last week. Too much coffee
shakes my grip, the camera, makes images
blurry, the spruce grouse a brown streak. Sorry.
Believe me, the red combs above its eyes raged,
almost burned me, almost set the forest
alight. That's right, it was early morning,
I hadn't slept and the dew was less
heavy than the fog. There was no warning,
no calling, and I didn't see the root
over which I tripped, nor the crossing,
nor the culvert, though the sound trickled through
my ears. Weary, I heard something passing
close by, swore it was my soul taking leave
and there it was, a grouse in the leaves.

5.

And there it is. A grouse in the leaves
uncovers the unfashionable
Romantic, so rural and lost I wave
at my own reflection, pull the wool
tight around my neck and shiver at how
old the ripples make me look, how tired
I am, lame, trying to walk like Thoreau
and my Thoreauvian friends. A liar
must do much better than this, be much
more than a body given to pauses
to search through the field guide for a match.
The Latin name of this bird amazes
naturalists no end, so I'll act astonished
until I believe I'm astonished.

6.

Until I believe I'm astonished
I will stand here and suffer. I promised
myself I'd be more awake, attuned, pushed
aside branches, woods and ruins, but a mist
has settled in the low spots like mist does.
Spring is beautiful. I use beautiful
too much, more than allowed, just because
petulance contains a single petal,
and that's enough to bring forth the flower.
It blooms. A curse, this lack of subtlety.
Like the marsh marigold, it's pure
poison. That nectar summons flies and bees
and me! Things grow cruel in the perennial
surface runoff, the ephemeral pool.

131

7.
Surface runoff. The ephemeral pool.
Call it what you like. I'm up to my boot-
tops in snow melt, up to my ears in fools
who go on as if nothing else could suit
this April night. Perhaps the frogs are right
for here I stand in the cold among them,
too human to be any good, midnight
pressing certain stars into my brainstem.
It's calm now. The big dipper handles breath
gently, turns and washes it. True. The grave
forest covers up every little death
with another. I die a bit each day
behind this mask. The heart freezes and thaws,
pulsing darkness. A chorus without pause.

from *Canadian Poetries*
published in *Best Canadian Poetry 2015*

DAVID SEYMOUR ☙

Song for the Call of the Richardson's Ground Squirrel Whose Call is a Song for the Cry of the Short-Eared Owlet (They May One Day Meet for Dinner)

In the cow pasture across the road, it may simply be
a trick of the light, an eyelash trapping the dusk.
They seem there, and there, and there and then gone.
Prairie mirages. But the call is unmistakable—
syncope of blue sky, fear, and the Swainson's Hawk's
lethal dive. Jazz interruptions in a calm Saskatchewan evening.
Nothing anyone can say is more humourless. Imagine
three cats in a bag. High-pitched, furry whoopee
cushions, a litany of helium balloons wheezing
out their last. Jack-knives puncturing the tires
on the bastard neighbour's unmufflered Datsun.
It's alarming enough to make you want to run home
and count the kids. Who knows? With such fleet, thieves' hands
perhaps they're only lamenting their lack of pockets
before ducking back into invisible kingdoms;
what choruses and sudden confusions, casualties,
among the families in those dark territories.
When you live for so long beneath the horizon
there must only be a language of weeping.
Listen as they peer partially, cautiously
back into the sunset world.

from *The Malahat Review*
published in *Best Canadian Poetry 2008*

SUE SINCLAIR ෫

Cherry Trees

A blur of white, pre-photogenic.
Ships bound for distant shores.

A hint of nostalgia
that isn't an escape—or if it is,
we escape only into the here and now,
only into this same place
cast in another light.

The trees stand unblinking,
pull down so much sunshine they seem
finally to disappear into it, become
a deficiency, pale, forgetful.
They gather absence around them
and are strangely increased by it
in a way I envy.

It feels like someone has put their head
on my shoulder. And it weighs
nothing at all.

from *PRISM international*
published in *Best Canadian Poetry 2010*

BARDIA SINAEE ◌

Escape from Statuary

It's no secret that some people wish they had a tail.
We're torn one by one from rolls of human Scotch tape
to be born. Why let anger dam your heart
and turn you into stone? Sunlight, rain is sorry.
Dark cloud, go study for the flood.

Congratulations! Your every whim brings light
to new dimensions. Even your farts are radiant blossoms
in the infrared dreamscape of the common vampire bat.

The human heart, despite its plumbing
and catalogue of attachments, can't signal before it turns
and must be followed closely if we wish to fly.
Helium, that frisky hothead and life of every party,
is running out. Why? Maybe you ask too many questions.
Maybe it's time to let the wind have your clothes.

from *Arc Poetry Magazine*
published in *Best Canadian Poetry 2015*

KAREN SOLIE ❧

Tractor

More than a storey high and twice that long,
it looks igneous, the Buhler Versatile 2360,
possessed of the ecology of some hellacious
minor island on which options
are now standard. Cresting the sections
in a corona part dirt, part heat, it appears
risen full-blown from our deeper needs,
aspiring its turbo-cooled air, articulated
and fully compatible. What used to take a week
it does in a day on approximately
a half-mile to the gallon. It cost one hundred
fifty grand. We hope to own it outright by 2017.
Few things wrought by human hands
are more sublime than the Buhler Versatile 2360.

Across the road, a crew erects the floodlit
derricks of a Texan outfit whose presumptions
are consistently vindicated.
The ancient sea bed will be fractured to 1000 feet
by pressuring through a pipe literal tons
of a fluid—the constituents of which
are best left out of this—
to tap the sweet gas where it lies like the side
our bread is buttered on. The earth shakes
terribly then, dear Houston, dear parent
corporation, with its re-broken dead and freshly
killed, the air concussive, cardiac, irregular.
It silences the arguments of every living thing
and our minds in that time are not entirely elsewhere.

But I was speaking of the Buhler Versatile 2360
Phase D! And how well recognized it is among the classics: Wagner,
Steiger, International Harvester, John Deere, Case,
Minneapolis-Moline, Oliver, White, Allis-Chalmers,
Massey-Ferguson, Ford, Rite, Rome.
One could say it manifests fate, cast
like a pearl around the grit of centuries. That,

in a sense, it's always been with us,
the diesel smell of a foregone conclusion.
In times of doubt, we cast our eyes
upon the Buhler Versatile 2360
and are comforted. And when it breaks down, or thinks
itself in gear and won't, for our own good, start,
it takes a guy out from the city at 60 bucks an hour
plus travel and parts, to fix it.

from *The Walrus*
published in *Best Canadian Poetry 2009*

CARMINE STARNINO ❧

Courtship

I threw myself at you,
my bald bachelor.
We binged
on eye contact.
Fell into bed, nuzzling.
So in love
we hardly slept.
The night light
did you proud
as you rode pillion
on my chest.
You woke afraid,
and I held you.
Biscuit nose,
fruitgum fingers.
Toe to head, you never
tasted better.
I declare this
on one knee,
my bonnie boy.

from *CV2*
published in *Best Canadian Poetry 2014*

RICARDO STERNBERG ✸

Blues

Toot me something on your golden horn
he said to the musician.
I feel cold as my soul turns blue.

Jerryrig me an intricate song
full of those diminished sevenths
and just enough thrust to push me through

bar by smoky bar, into oblivion.
Extricate me from thorny feelings,
put brain and heart to sleep.

Bring out a flute and its Bolivian
so sorrow can be trumped by sorrow.
Afford me, at any price, some peace.

Today I am bedeviled
befogged by this predictment:
will I find myself myself again tomorrow?

from *The Fiddlehead*
published in *Best Canadian Poetry 2012*

BRUCE TAYLOR ☙

Little Animals

On bokes for to rede I me delyt.

1

That old book has a million moving parts,
and when you open it to look inside,
they all spill out, like the escapement
from a sproinged clock,
spelling up the life and correspondence
of a Dutch cloth merchant called van Leeuwenhoek.
A regular little factory, this book,
as busy as a Jacquard loom
constructing its bustling world
of high-piled clouds and shambling
courtyards and canals,
and copper gutters filling up with rain,
a 17th-century rain, curled
like a great cascading periwig
over the cankered rooftiles of old Delft.

It has some chickens in it, and a hive of bees
and 16 coffin-bearers and a bowl,
(and divers things too numerous to name).
Press your eye against the page
and marvel at the makes that shift
this pretty engine, with its
weights and wormscrews,
tumbling cams and pins,
all shaped by hand & cunningly contrived
to move a miniature Dutchman through his life.

2

He was the first Microscopist,
a worldly man compelled
by wasteful curiosity to build
a homely magnifier and enlarge
inconsequential items: fishscales,
pepper, fly-stings, dandruff, dust,
nose hair, spidersilk, some stuff
he found between his teeth,
and he was the first to do a thing
the finest intellects of Europe never thought of,
which was to look, to simply look,
inside a water drop

at all the thrashing whiptailed swimmers,
motile cogs and quaking ghosts
that make their lives in there,
and these he called his "little animals,"
some appearing in the glass
"as large as your arm" and others,
"as small as the beard hairs of a man
that hath not in a fortnight shaved,"
disporting themselves with merry
convolutions, flexing their numerous
limbs and nimble paws
in a manner pleasing to a haberdasher's eye,
commendatory to the Genius
of their Maker.

3

So, here was a man who looked
at pieces of his world and found
more worlds inside them,
which is the natural order: worlds
that roost in tiny apertures on worlds
where dainty worldlings
dwell, and each one
is a world as well, some

milling in the streets of Delft and others,
pulsing through pondwater.
And each of these should have a book.
And there should be a book
for every punctuation mark
in all those books, and every speck
should be recorded and preserved
so that all things in time might be
made known and magnified
and put before us in the book of books.

But for now there is only this excellent one
by Clifford Dobell to enjoy,
and I have neglected to mention
the best part, which is the bookplate pasted
on its inside cover, ornately framed
in the Art Nouveau style,
and the picture inside it
which hangs in a well-lit stillness,
calm and perplexing as a tarot card,
over a rippling armorial ribbon
bearing a line from Chaucer.

It is a scene from mythical Arcadia, not
the prefecture of modern Greece,
but the literary, made-up place
where idle minds imagine
poetry belongs: sloping pastures
on unpopulated hills,
a billowing meringue of clouds
stitched with careful penstrokes,
a lonely place, at once
intimate and remote, for this
is a private wilderness, a place
for nobody to find but me,
and curled up at the bottom
of a vine-laden sycamore sits
a boyish short-horned faun, his hooves
tucked up beneath him, and instead
of scamping through purple freshets,
"trilling joyously on oaten pipe,"

or humping dryads, as it may be,
in a dappled grove,
the little goat is captivated by
a book too small to read the title of,
and look how he holds it, his book,
exactly as I hold mine, his head
a little tilted, one hand propping up his chin,
the picture of perfect absorption,
a picture of life at its best,
because, what else is there to do
in Paradise but loaf beneath a tree,
and dream of other worlds?

4

Or peer for hours and hours,
and more hours adding up to years,
through bits of polished glass
at beings who have no idea
they are being watched?

5

A spring rain pools on the porch-chairs
at the group home for addicts,
and the same rain soaks a toddler's sock
that has been lying in my yard all year
and this is the very rain
that fills a frog pond down the road
where I go to collect little animals
to look at in my microscope.
It is all I have done this week.
I am neglecting my life
to spy on theirs! And if I had a shop that sold
button loops and red kersey
and bombazine at 9 stivers an ell,
that shop would surely fail,
with no one there to watch the till,
for you would find me locked upstairs instead

in a rambling sun-stunned room,
the room where Vermeer himself
might well have painted
our hero in his scholar's robe, with his
star globe and dividers
and his cabinet of handmade
brass and silver microscopes, a man
of his time, staring until the light ran out at things
not mentioned in the Bible.

And I am a man of my time, but my
microscope came here from China
in a foam box reeking of solvents,
and the first live thing I saw in it
was a piece of myself, a tiny monster
from the back of my tongue: a macrophage,
whose role in my life is to eat
my enemies, the black
jots and whits, the lithe and vibrating
umlauts, hyphens & tildes that would use me for food—
and that is where you will find Narcissus
today, gazing down at himself
on a clean glass slide,
on which a nano-assassin
encapsulated in a see-through sphere
is taking care of business, and there
in its scintillant middle I could see
my would-be devourers
being devoured, a pleasing sight.
And the next thing I looked at was yogurt.
And then, I walked out to the pond.

6

On the path to the pond
there's a hole, fairly large,
where a pope-faced turtle old enough
to be my grandmother buried her eggs
last year. It is littered with leathery
shells and I have a strong urge

to fill up my pockets with these,
but it is not what I came for. The place
where I gather my samples
reminds me of a ruined Roman
amphitheatre, there are trees all around it
frozen in gestures of theatrical
menace and operatic grief.
A private wilderness, but the air here
is not quiet, it is shrill with sex,
the unceasing, imperious, loud need
of these treefrogs insisting on sex.
There is skim-ice on the water,
still, and there are animals under there, too,
demanding sex, and in truth
I would not refuse it myself,
if some girl with a high forehead
rinsed in the silvery light of old Delft
were to stop pouring milk
or reading her mail
and come out to the musky woods
where a goat-footed stranger is waiting.
But now, I must open a hole in the ice
with my long-handled spoon
and scoop out a helping of murk
to fill my bowl.

7

It is water, the restless stuff
that sustains and dissolves us,
and I tell you, though you will never
believe what I say, it is alive inside,
for there are animals within it
smaller even than the mites
upon the rind of a cheese,
"and their motions in water
are so swift and various,
upwards, downwards, and round about
that it is wonderful to see."
For it is down in the grey

and mazy darkness of the pond
that they are constructing their
glittering clattertrap City of Madness,
with its glass ladders, and lemon-green
spirals and a sky traversed by
delirious weirdos, one
like an angry emoticon, with two long hairs
embrangled on its scalp,
one like a revolving cocklebur,
and another like an animated spill,
(as if an accident could live!)
and crescent moons and popeyed gorgons, things
with knives for hands,
frenetic writhers, tumblers, bells
on stalks, a sort of great loose
muscle flinching and contracting,
diatoms like crystalline
canoes serenely gliding
down a coast of brown decay, and suddenly,
what looks to be a throbbing bronze
Victrola trumpet
rocketing around as if it won the war!
And you can almost hear the fanfare
as it plants its small end in a clump of muck
and starts to stretch itself,
and stretch until it is
as long as an alp horn,
as long and quivering as a plume of smoke
as long and quivering and dreadful as a cyclone funnel,
working the furious hairs of its mouth to suck
its lessers down its throat.

8

I have stared at them all week
in my Chinese microscope and have tried
to absorb what I saw.
I have studied my little animals so closely,
and have memorized their names,
the names they received

from muttonchopped scholars in the age
of tailcoats and columnar hats, there was
lacrymaria olor, tears
of the swan, by which we mean
that it is somewhat tear-shaped, if a tear
should have a long prehensile neck
to wrap around its food,
and there was *stentor* the loudspeaker,
which speaks for itself,
rotaria rotatoria, named
for the whirling cartwheels on its mouth,
suctoria, because it sucks, *amoeba*
because it makes me sick,
digenea because, merciful God,
I have never seen anything like that,
and paramecium which slides
like a long grey shadow
through a world it knows by feel,
serene as a basking shark,
and takes what it needs
and gives nothing.

And there is no end to them,
no end in numbers,
and no end in strangeness,
no end to their appetites, and all of it
exactly as van Leeuwenhoek
described it to us all those years ago,
when he, being the first to *look*
became the first to see
that what the wise men said was wrong,
what gnaws at our lapsed and sinful
world is not death at all,
the old machinework mannequin
swinging his scythe, he is not there.
It is not Death that undresses us,

pulls at the loose threads,
teases our garments apart,
and thrusts itself down
to make more of itself inside us,

nor is it Death
that incises those lines
in our cheeks
and lays his corrupting touch
on a Dutch girl's breast,
or calls up to us
from the cool earth
under the ice-covered pond—

for if you look, simply look,
with your bit of ground glass
you will see what is eating
these holes in the world, what chews
at the black straggle
and clings to those rafts of algae,
and cries up from the pages of a
strange old book, and hangs
in the damp sycamores
hollering for sex, sex, sex,
and probes in the dark muck
with its snakelike head,
if that thing is its head,
then opens its sudden mouth
with its wheel of whirling hairs
and starts to pull one
world after another
into its throat.

from *Quarc* (a joint issue of *Arc Poetry Magazine* and *The New Quarterly)*
published in *Best Canadian Poetry 2012*

SOUVANKHAM THAMMAVONGSA ❧

Gayatri

I have a picture of us when we are seven
but we aren't in it. At the time it was taken

we thought we were. We posed with our wide
grins and best-friends-forever certainty. I angled

the camera to capture us in front of a Christmas tree.
All the sparkling tinsel and dangling silver balls aren't there.

There is only the ceiling and the tip
of the pine needle. There isn't a star or an angel

on top. I have kept this picture of us for years,
the only one to remember and laugh at what happened

to us then. It was taken before a time you could
see a picture on a screen, see how it turned out

and decide whether it was worth keeping. I think of you
now and again, the plain peanut butter sandwiches we ate

with apples. You said you were going to be a dentist
when you grew up, and with a fork and a spoon

you determined it was possible I would live
and sent me home with a bag full of Twizzlers and hair bands.

from *The Walrus*
published in *Best Canadian Poetry 2016*

SHARON THESEN ◌৪

My Education as a Poet

> *Where affliction conquers us with brute force, beauty*
> *sneaks in and topples the empire of the self from within.*
> —Simone Weil

(Dad, I dreamed about you last night. Mom showed me your stiff hand
open at the top of the bed and said "See?" I had to agree it was stiff and dead
alright. I was freaking out because I'd missed a meeting at work and was
relieved Dad had died so I'd have an excuse. But then he returns, is walking
around like nothing happened though he looks pale and frail and soon to die
again, possibly). He would sing,
Go to sleep my little pickaninnie
Underneath the silver sunny moon
Hushabye, lullaby, mama's little baby

and before that my grandmother's red coral brooch—
Grandma: pianist, good-time girl, Rosicrucian—
the brooch I lost one night at one of those parties
it took days to recover from, *beating myself up—*

the good lickins with wooden spoon with branch from Sacred Grove
with belt with whatever was to hand & we were lucky
because when the kids down the street were bad
they had to go find and present to their mom
their own stick for the good lickins they got at the Shuswap

their dad would walk out
into the lake holding up a bottle
in one hand, a glass in the other, and hoist himself
onto the raft, us on the beach
laughing & waving, he was an okay guy,
a great joke teller, I'd always listen hard from
the bedroom when I heard Bill's ice cubes quieten down

& he'd say "So okay a Jew and a Catholic
walk into a bar" but even better were the mysterious
filthy jokes that would emerge out from

stupefied silence at 3:30 in the morning
and the laughter was tired or maybe
there was some sort of decorum such as when
someone would leap across the living room
to light his wife's cigarette, *he was so in love with her*
my mother said, *she'd barely have the cigarette*
out of the package before he'd be over there with the lighter—
Poetry: a bright flame.
I always knew we were in for a long night
when Dad got the banjo out and ripped into *Bye Bye Blues*
& who knew how the evening would turn out,
in joy or in sorrow.

Sometimes the parties would take place at Bill's or
somewhere else in which case there might be a phone call
at 4 a.m. to come and drive them home even though I couldn't
drive yet so I'd walk over and get the keys,
just put it in Drive, Dad would say, & off we'd go
with the high beams on & the birds beginning to tweet.
Brett Enemark used to say this was Young Driver Training
in Prince George; he'd done it, too. At least they were being
responsible by not getting behind the wheel in a condition
Mom referred to as *tight*. This was poetry: terms like
getting tight.

Both Bill and Dad were good joke-tellers but Dad
a big fan of Bob Hope, had a more technical approach:
He'd study Hope's routine on the Ed Sullivan Show.
"Listen to this" he'd say, as we scrutinized the timing.
Dad could even imitate Bob Hope's little smile.

Poetry: timing, a little smile, the lyrics to *Ragtime Cowboy Joe*:
he's a high falutin', rootin' tootin', son of a gun
from Arizona! Dad would finish
with a flourish of his pick hand, whirling it around
like a pitcher on the mound, and give his little grin and
shake his head as if to say, Boy, that was fun! And reach
for his Bacardi & Coke.

He transferred mandolin-type playing to the banjo & worshipped
the guitar moves of Les Paul. I can still hear the wall-of-sound

playing and singing, a drone poured off the surface
of the tight harmony with Mary Ford. *The World is Waiting
for the Sunrise* was Dad's most soulful cover—
you'd hear him practicing in the basement, tiki lights
parsing the dark little bar.

Before that, in Kamloops, when grandma's piano arrived
after her death Dad drove me over the bridge for lessons.
My first piece was called "Indian Dance," a steady
single-note repetition on the left hand and a simple
two-note slightly sad yet menacing melody on the right.
Poetry: *something out of whack*. Grandma had played that same piano
for friends and guests both whites and Haida thirty years before
in Masset, accompanied on violin by her husband Edward.
It was known that in the hands of certain women, red cedar bark could be pounded
to a softness greater than cashmere. But most of those women
if not all of them were dead by then. Most of the artists, carvers, and poets were
dead by then also, or crippled by disease.
Mom's *biodad*, an O'Donnell, logging accountant and charmer,
drinker, brawler, persona non grata, left early on.
Her grandfather was then
her father until he died when she was seven, and then
tubercular Edward arrived from Germany with his violin and soon
he died too. *Poetry: consumption and epitaph.*

Mom would be homesick for the sound
of the canneries and salty crashing ocean,
kelp and sand dunes north of Masset
toward Rose Spit where Raven discovered Humans.
Every Christmas a dozen cans of Alaska King crabmeat
would arrive from what she called The Islands.
She'd tumbled down the white dunes & gone out after storms
with a can opener to see what had washed up from shipwrecks:
mostly pork and beans. *Poetry: a can opener.* Treasures
were the glass buoys—large, pocked, thick-glassed orbs
from the Japanese fishing fleets out somewhere in the
four thousand miles of open sea to the west of Rose Spit.
In the sanatorium Mom was homesick for fresh fish
but forced to eat cream straight from the cow,
she and her friend from The Islands both at death's door
in young womanhood with children at home later sent

Haida bracelets for Xmas—mine was Dogfish Woman
crafted by someone whose signature was "XX" and
whose carving was a bit off on an angle. *Poetry:*
off on an angle amidst the TB and the whalers and the moieties.

from *Arc Poetry Magazine*
published in *Best Canadian Poetry 2014*

SARAH YI-MEI TSIANG ೞ

Visit

I saw my father yesterday,
Sitting on the wall of his mausoleum.
He held my hand and told me he forgave me
and I asked, for what?

He smelled of apples, an autumn of leaves
for skin. I remember you like this, I said,
a harvest—an orchard of a man.

He opened his shirt, plucked a plum
from his lungs and held it out to me.
Everything, he said, is a way of remembering.

from *Arc Poetry Magazine*
published in *Best Canadian Poetry 2013*

PRISCILA UPPAL ✂

To My Suicidal Husband

Please do not look for poetry
in your death. Your drowning or
hanging or tsunami of pills & booze
will not be poetic.

There is no residue of poetry
in a bloated cheek snagged by a fish hook,
in a cracked leather belt swaying
from a light fixture or in a sludge of vomit
protruding from your throat like a second tongue.

And certainly no poetry will fall
upon your devastated wife folding
the last pairs of your dirty underwear &
ignoring the phone on a Saturday night,
piles of pizza crusts on the coffee table,
one of your horror films running aimlessly
on the screen, wondering why you
never imagined her twitching hands,
the packing up of your extensive library,
or the signed book of your own poems,
To Priscila, my love, because nothing exists
without you, under her lumpy pillow, now
warm as soggy shoes left to dry in the sun, and
her sobbing the last of her suspect memories
of your tender eyes, your brisk, hunched
gait, the slow circling of your hands
across her belly, into the awful emptiness of
hangers, towels and toothbrush holders,
microwavable meals and refrigerator
reminders, because your imagination
failed to reconcile the oxymorons
of her & your death.

This is not poetry.
Trust me.
While I am still your wife, and not a warning.

There is nothing less poetic than your death.
And nothing more plain.

from *Cordite Poetry Review*
published in *Best Canadian Poetry 2015*

ZACHARIAH WELLS ☙

One and One

For every one there is a one, and one
and one make one, divided.

For every one a one must die, and every
death is one, provided

every other is a one and one
is every other.

An other and a one make one,
husbanded and brided.

The union of a one and one
makes other, suicided.

Self-murder of the one-in-one is mother
of the other one and one

another's one-in-ones conspire to smother
other ones, while lovers

wire their one and ones
implacably together.

One is bound and gagged by one, one
saws and frays the knot

of one, and one
lets slip the tether.

after George Herbert

from *The Winnipeg Review*
published in *Best Canadian Poetry 2012*

PATRICIA YOUNG ✀

July Baby

Why can't we be more like the dandelion,
hollow-stemmed, milky-sapped?
Wouldn't sex be sexier if sex were asexual?
Just because we possess
stamens and pistils
doesn't mean
we have to use them.
Let's fertilize ourselves.
What's the evolutionary advantage
of going ga-ga and wobbly in the knees?
Don't you get tired of the complex human complexities?
Why can't we travel
all night on an all-night train
and wake up as something else, a taproot, say.
Let's be savvy and adaptive and flaunt
our tiny florets. Wouldn't you rather
by-pass the awkward introductions
and clone yourself ?
Don't think *invasive weed*,
think *fairy clock, rosette of deeply-lobed leaves*.
It might be fun to pop up
unwelcome and anywhere,
the front lawn of City Hall.
Why can't we be more like the humble
dandelion in a field of humble dandelions?
Who says you can't throw off
your body and float like a filament
in the summer wind? Let's get drunk
as puffballs in a roadside ditch.
Let's make summer babies without reproductive organs
or classes in synchronized breathing.
Three days old, this one lies on a blanket
beneath the maple tree. Oh prince
of the meadow, oh bright
yellow flower-head!

from *Maisonneuve*
published in *Best Canadian Poetry 2009*

CHANGMING YUAN ☙

Awaiting

There is a long wait of the passengers
For the detouring and delayed bus
And the wait of the wintry grasses

The wait of the legendary lion king
Before it preys upon a real baby zebra
And the wait of the summer sun deep in the nightmare

The wait of the orchid on the window ledge
The wait of the diamond in an unknown mine
And the wait where you stop and watch

And there is a wait of this darkness
Which you are going to compress into words
A wait that is to spread out thin on the blank paper

Unlike winter stars holding their light in light-years
The wait after you finish writing
And the longer wait then

from *The Dalhousie Review*
published in *Best Canadian Poetry 2012*

JAN ZWICKY ❧

from **Practising Bach**

for performance with Bach's E Major Partita for Solo Violin, BWV1006

Prelude

There is, said Pythagoras, a sound
the planet makes: a kind of music
just outside our hearing, the proportion
and the resonance of things—not
the clang of theory or the wuthering
of human speech, not even
the bright song of sex or hunger, but
the unrung ringing that
supports them all.

The wife, no warning, dead
when you come home. Ducats
in the fishheads that you salvage
from the rubbish heap. Is the cosmos
laughing at us? No. It's saying

improvise. Everywhere you look
there's beauty, and it's rimed
with death. If you find injustice
you'll find humans, and this means
that if you listen, you'll find love.
The substance of the world is light,
is water: here, clear
even when it's dying; even when the dying
seems unbearable, it runs.

from *Vallum*
published in *Best Canadian Poetry 2009*

CONTRIBUTORS' COMMENTARY AND BIOGRAPHIES ✑

MARGARET AVISON died in July 2007 in Toronto. Her work has, over the course of a career spanning four decades, won numerous awards, including two Governor General's Awards and, for *Concrete and Wild Carrot*, the Griffin Poetry Prize. Her books of poetry include *Always Now: The Collected Poems* and *Momentary Dark*. Her final collection, *Listening: The Last Poems of Margaret Avison*, was published posthumously by McClelland & Stewart in spring, 2009.

In a gently humorous way, Margaret confesses her aversion to generalities, contrasting them with particulars, the "particulates" whom she loves to "dance" among, with "castanets" in her poetry.

KEN BABSTOCK lives in Toronto. He is the author of *Mean* (1999), winner of the Atlantic Poetry Prize and Milton Acorn Award, *Days into Flatspin* (2001), winner of a K.M. Hunter Award and shortlisted for the Winterset Prize, *Airstream Land Yacht* (2006), which won the Trillium Award for Poetry, and *Methodist Hatchet*, which won the 2012 Griffin Prize for Poetry. Babstock's poems have been translated into Dutch, German, French, and Serbo-Croatian.

Of "Autumn News from the Donkey Sanctuary," Babstock writes, "As birthday gift to a friend, we had 'adopted' a donkey at a sanctuary near Guelph, Ont. Subsequently, newsletters began arriving in the mail so it was like being sent a Wallace Stevens title minus its accompanying poem. Gift begets gift. It likely opens too close to derivative Stevens, with the named 'characters' singing, or chanting, but the intent was to drift near to political allegory while avoiding any single interpretive trap. Agamben's thoughts on Homo Sacer float nearby, and by implication critiques of western liberalism's more explicit shortcomings, but also surveillance and safety and domesticity and verse. I very nearly dumped this poem before noticing its screeching turn arrives approximately where it would in a sonnet. So, I don't know, levels of illusion embedded in the pastoral. Have finally visited the sanctuary, and am happy to report... (?)"

JOHN WALL BARGER was born in New York City and grew up in Halifax, Nova Scotia. He has published three collections with Palimpsest Press. The most recent, *The Book of Festus*, was a finalist for the 2016 J.M. Abraham Poetry Award. He was co-winner of *The Malahat Review*'s 2017 Long Poem Prize.

Of "Urgent Message from the Captain of the Unicorn Hunters," Barger writes, "I came across the word 'auk' in *Ulysses* (Leopold Bloom is drowsing: 'Going to dark bed there was a square round Sinbad the Sailor roc's auk's egg in the night of the bed of all the auks of the rocs of Darkinbad the Brightdayler') and looked it up: an extinct bird. The great auk was a black and white flightless bird, a metre tall, with tiny wings, hunted for millennia for its feathers, pelt, meat, oil, and large eggs. The last one seen in Britain was on the islet of Stac an Armin, St Kilda, Scotland, in July 1844. Three local men tied it up and kept it alive for three days, till a storm appeared. Believing the great auk to be a witch causing the storm, they killed it with a stick. My poem arose out of a desire to have a conversation with those three men. It is also just about unicorns."

JOHN BARTON lives in Victoria. His eleven books of poetry and seven chapbooks include *West of Darkness: Emily Carr, a Self-Portrait* (third bilingual edition, 2006), *Hypothesis* (2001), *Hymn* (2009), *Balletomane* (2012), *For the Boy with the Eyes of the Virgin: Selected Poems* (2012), *Polari* (2014), and *Reframing Paul Cadmus* (2016). Co-editor of *Seminal: The Anthology of Canada's Gay-Male Poets* (2007), he is compiling *The Essential Douglas LePan*. He edits *The Malahat Review*.

Barton writes, "During the Second World War, Alan Turing (1912-1954), considered one of the great scientific thinkers of the twentieth century, broke the Enigma Code that allowed the Allies to gain a winning advantage over Germany by being able to eavesdrop on the Nazis' encrypted military communications. Turing also made significant advances in mathematical thinking that laid the foundation for the development of the present-day computer. However, in 1952, he was convicted of illegal homosexual acts under the United Kingdom's Offences against the Person Act, the same statute under which Oscar Wilde had been successfully prosecuted almost sixty years earlier. Turing could not cite his contributions during the war in his own defense because they were considered state secrets. In 1954, he died of cyanide poisoning; the subsequent inquest determined that he died by his own hand, though many felt his death was accidental. 'Turing's Machine' began with the epigraph's use of repetition and variation and how an obvious illogic belies its apparent simplicity and literalness. The recursive nature of the pantoum seemed an ideal way to plumb its plainspoken contradictions and to capture something of Turing's thought and predicament. A structure based on constantly repeating lines captures something of the obsessive, if/if-not, zero-and-one qualities of machine code. The poem's language is software while its form is hardware, and I have attempted to push the permutations of both as far as possible in order to convey the artificiality of hetero-normative thinking and the tragic absurdity entrapping men, great and ordinary, in the mid-twentieth century."

SHIRLEY BEAR was born on the Tobique First Nation. She is an original member of the Wabnaki language group of New Brunswick. Bear is a multimedia artist, writer, and traditional First Nation herbalist and elder. She was the 2002 recipient of the New Brunswick Arts Board's Excellence in the Arts Award, and her writing has been included in several anthologies, including *The Colour of Resistance: A Contemporary Collection of Writing by Aboriginal Women* (Sister Vision, 1998). In 2006, McGilligan Books published her collection of art, poetry, and political writing, *Virgin Bones/Belayak Kcikug'nas'ikn'ug*. In 2011 she was named to the Order of Canada.

Of "Flight," Bear writes, "A lover once bathed in a cold stream for me. It was the most erotic event and the first time anyone ever did this, for me to enjoy. I used to write notes, appointments, birthdays, and sketched in my day minder. It was a convenient sort of 'all in one.' When I was asked to submit some work to the *West Coast LINE 45*, I re-discovered this poem in one of my many day minders. From my studio in 1000 Parker St., Vancouver, I incorporated the present with the past when I submitted the poem and found that it was magical."

YVONNE BLOMER lives in Victoria, where she is the city's poet laureate. Her most recent books include *Sugar Ride: Cycling from Hanoi to Kuala Lumpur* (Palimpsest, 2017) and *As if a Raven* (Palimpsest, 2014). In the fall of 2017 *Refugium: Poems for the Pacific* which Yvonne edited will be released with Caitlin Press. Yvonne holds an MA in Creative Writing with distinction from the University of East Anglia, UK.

Blomer writes, "'The Roll Call to the Ark' is a poem taken out of a series of poems called *The Birds of the Bible*. The poem is in two voices and was inspired by Genesis where first Noah is instructed to take two of each kind of male and female of every animal on to the ark and then later is instructed to take seven of clean and one of unclean animals."

STEPHANIE BOLSTER was born in Vancouver and raised in Burnaby, BC. She has published four books of poetry, the first of which, *White Stone: The Alice Poems*, won the Governor General's and the Gerald Lampert Awards in 1998. She was honoured to edit the inaugural *The Best Canadian Poetry in English* in 2008 and is honoured once again to see her work appear here. She teaches creative writing at Concordia University in Montréal.

Of "Gardening," Bolster writes, "I'd rather write poems about gardens than do the work a garden requires, a preference I was forced to confront after moving to a suburb. Add an infestation of white grubs, a lifelong squeamishness about squirmy things, and a writing project that required me to interrogate my equally lifelong fascination with the intersection of the made and the natural, and I ended up with what would become this poem. I made up the foxgloves, though I can no longer remember why I believed the poem needed them. (Something, perhaps, about the fact that they are ubiquitous intruders in my parents' garden, that they are both beautiful and poisonous, and that the word in itself offers a Beatrix Potter-esque suggestion of that intersection of the made and the natural.) I've also forgotten how many drafts this poem went through, though I know there were more than enough to reaffirm my admiration for Pound's winnowing down of 'In a Station of the Metro.' I know, too, that without Alison Strumberger having solicited my work for the 'Wild' issue of *Branch* (thank you, Alison!), this little poem would have remained in the darkness of my hard drive for a long time, if not forever."

TIM BOWLING lives in Edmonton. His twentieth book, *The Heavy Bear* (Wolsak and Wynn, 2017), is a novel in which the three main characters are the ghosts of Delmore Schwartz and Buster Keaton, and a material poet named Tim Bowling.

Bowling writes, "I wrote 'Union Local 64' out of two impulses: a disgust with systems of all kinds, and a great respect and love for my parents, who were raised during the Depression and had to leave high school to find work."

ASA BOXER lives in Montreal. His poetry has garnered several prizes and is included in various anthologies around the world. His books are *The Mechanical Bird* (Signal, 2007), *Skullduggery* (Signal, 2011), *Friar Biard's Primer to the New World* (Frog Hollow Press, 2013), and *Etymologies* (Anstruther Press, 2016). Boxer is founder and manager of the Montreal International Poetry Prize.

Of "Dante's Ikea," Boxer writes, "Any resemblance between Ikea and the Inferno is purely coincidental. For one, Virgil wouldn't be caught dead at Ikea. There are no three-headed dogs at the door. There are far more circles in hell. And you don't need a boat to get around."

JULIE BRUCK is from Montreal and lives in San Francisco. Her fourth collection, *How to Avoid Huge Ships* (Brick Books) is forthcoming in 2018. Recent work has appeared in *Plume*, *The New Yorker*, *The Puritan*, and *The Academy of American Poets' Poem-A-Day*, Her latest book, *Monkey Ranch* (Brick Books), received the 2012 Governor General's Literary Award for Poetry.

Bruck writes, "'Two Fish' just flopped into my lap one day, like an ugly bottomfeeder. At first, I didn't know what to make of it, but when I read it at a Christian college in Ontario and half-jokingly challenged the audience to tell me what it was about, somebody said it was 'obviously about God.' That made me take another, less flippant (no pun intended) look at the poem. For the record, we did have two fish, and the younger fish died recently, but not from neglect. She was eleven years old, and was very well-loved. Now we have one fish."

ANNE CARSON was born in Canada and teaches ancient Greek for a living.

Of "Father's Old Blue Cardigan," Carson writes, "This was my mother's favourite poem I ever wrote. She submitted it to the monthly newsletter of the care facility where my father spent his last years (The Pines in Bracebridge, Ontario) and when they published it she xeroxed the page and had it laminated so as to show it to everyone who came to our house."

PETER CHIYKOWSKI writes and draws in Toronto. His work as a cartoonist, humourist, and poet has appeared or made mention in *Entertainment Weekly*, *Newsweek*, MTV.com, *Huffington Post*, *Buzzfeed*, and *The Globe and Mail*. He has published three collections of his original Aurora Award-winning webcomic *Rock, Paper, Cynic* and posts material every week at rockpapercynic.com.

Of "Notes from the Canary Islands," Chiykowski writes, "Long distance relationships are a test of a couple's emotional ductility, their ability to be drawn out thinner and thinner, to resonate with a higher and higher pitch until they reach a sticking point. This poem came about through just this kind of psychological metallurgy. My partner had been studying in England for months, messaging me sporadically from a house whose lead pipes frazzled her wireless internet connection, when I began to wonder what happens to all of the affection that gets lost across the massive distances of international communication."

GEORGE ELLIOTT CLARKE, the Africadian poet, hails from Three Mile Plains, Nova Scotia. Now a University of Toronto professor, Clarke has published seventeen poetry works, including an epic, debuting with *Canticles I (MMXVI)* and *Canticles I (MMXVII)*, and won numerous awards, including two Governor General's Awards.

Clarke writes, "Blame Aristotle. The classical Greek philosopher's treatise, *Poetics*, preaches that lyric poetry is good, tragic (dramatic) poetry superior, and epic poetry most divine. Though I'm a bo'n Africadian and a publishing poet since 1978, I've always trusted Aristotle's vision. I've written lyric and narrative poetry, plus verse tragedy and comedy, plus libretti for opera. But now—since February 2008, starting out in Zanzibar—I've undertaken an epic poem: 'The Canticles.' My subject is two-fold: 1) The five-century debate—pro and con—over the African Slave Trade and 'White-Man's-Burden' imperialism; 2) the image of the 'African' in Western civilization. I'm drafting (principally) free-verse, dramatic monologues that present speakers, either historical or imaginary: thus, a 'Negress' attacks Napoleon; or Elizabeth Barrett Browning explains that she'd feared to marry Robert because of the risk she'd bear him a 'Negro' child. I've given myself rules: I must write with real, fountain-pen ink, but not write anything in Toronto, where I live. So, 'The Canticles' are travelling—if not travelogue—poetry. 'A Letter from Henry Tucker, August 28, 1789,' was written in Southampton, Bermuda, on March 30, 2012, following research I did at the library in the island's capital city, Hamilton. My 'letter' draws on those I found in a historical article about relations between Nova Scotia and Bermuda. The incidents described did happen, apparently, including Mrs. Tucker's confusion over her husband's 'race,' if not his 'sex.'"

DON COLES was born in Woodstock, ON, and lives in Toronto. He has published a number of poetry collections in Canada, one (translated into German by Margitt Lehbert) in Germany, one in the U.K. *Forests of the Medieval World* won the Governor General's Award for Poetry in 1993, *Kurgan* won the Trillium Book Prize in 2000 (the last year in which there was only one such award), and *For the Living and the Dead* (a translation of the poetry of the Swedish poet Tomas Tranströmer) won the John Glassco Prize for best literary translation in 1996.

ANNE COMPTON lives in Rothesay, NB. A poet, essayist, editor, and anthologist, she is the author of four books of poetry, including *Processional*, winner of the Governor General's Award for Poetry in 2005. She is the recipient of The Lieutenant-Governor's Award for High Achievement in the Arts (2014) and The Alden Nowlan Award for Excellence in the Literary Arts (2008). Her most recent book is *Afterwork: Essays on Literature and Beauty* (2017).

Of "Stars, Sunday Dawn," Compton writes, "The speaker of the poem is the younger sister of a boy who is an avid runner, especially on Sundays, the day of the week free from chores. He's turned every room of the house into a racecourse, but on Sundays he races—and she clocks him—in the biggest building on the farm, the granary. The poem pivots on the image of the girl holding the stopwatch. I've always thought running and writing a lot alike: both alter time. Obviously, in the course of this narrative poem, something happens to the boy."

DANI COUTURE was raised on four Canadian military bases and currently lives in Toronto. She is the author of three collections of poetry and the novel *Algoma* (Invisible Publishing). *Sweet* was shortlisted for the Trillium Book Award for Poetry and won the ReLit Award for Poetry. Her most recent collection is *Yaw* (Mansfield Press, 2014).

Of "Salvage," Couture writes, "I lived on the edge of the Detroit River for years. My family still does. The constant backdrop to my days there was a combination of weather, water, and freighters. The ships pass day and night, only stopping for the annual winter lay-up. As a teenager, I chose a favourite shipping line the way one chooses a favourite baseball or hockey team. As an adult, my first novel was named after that same shipping line. Edward Burtynsky's "Shipbreaking" series was an influence on this poem, as was the *Edwin H. Gott*, one of thirteen 1000-footers that sail the Great Lakes."

LUCAS CRAWFORD was born in Halifax, raised in rural Nova Scotia, spent a decade away from the Maritimes (in Edmonton, Montreal, and Vancouver), and now lives in Fredericton. Lucas wrote *Sideshow Concessions* (Invisible 2015), which won the Robert Kroetsch Award for Innovative Poetry, as well as a research monograph entitled *Transgender Architectonics* (Routledge 2016). As an assistant professor at the University of New Brunswick, Lucas researches fat, food, transgender, and the twentieth-century British novel.

Of "Failed Séances for Rita MacNeil (1944-2013)," Crawford writes, "I drafted this poem in 2012 as part of a pair. Rita MacNeil owned a tearoom in Nova Scotia. 'Tearoom' was also a word used in some urban queer communities to denote public spaces where sex happens. As a queer small-town Nova Scotian, I am attached to both definitions of 'tearoom' and wanted to show that they might not be so unrelated. If public sex is about deciding that you ought to feel entitled to do unsanctioned things in the public sphere, well, there is scarcely anything less acceptable than being an unrepentant fat woman with a complex history who dares to take the stage and put her body on display. A year later, Rita died, and my upset led me to rewrite the poem. It was immediately clear that the Rita poem needed to 'fly on [its] own,' to quote one of her songs. I was a young fat girl for whom 'Rita MacNeil fat jokes' were not an uncommon presence. Now, as a genderqueer person living far from home, I felt a number of losses reverberate through Rita's death. I could not speak to her, but I wanted there to be a public record of her fatness being experienced as something that strengthened someone else, and in an unpredictable way. These are séances written by a person who doesn't quite believe in spirits, so the extent to which they 'fail' is uncertain. Instead of reaching Rita, I'm speaking to readers. Can a reader of poetry manifest a lost icon?"

LORNA CROZIER was born in Saskatchewan but now lives on Vancouver Island. An Officer of the Order of Canada, she's published seventeen books of poetry. In 2016 *The Wrong Cat* won her third Pat Lowther Award for the best book of poems by a Canadian woman. Her latest book, *What the Soul*

Doesn't Want, came out in the spring of 2017. She's read on every continent except Antarctica.

Of "Seeing My Father in the Neighbours' Cockatoo," Crozier writes, "Our first neighbours on Vancouver Island, an older couple who befriended us, owned a blind dog who navigated their house and yard by smell, and a cockatoo who screamed most of the day and stripped its breast of feathers. The couple loved their pets and treated them well, but cockatoos that self-mutilate do so out of depression brought on by loneliness. One day the bird looked at me with my father's eyes. It was a startling moment of connection and it initiated the poem. That look led me to wonder about the reappearance of those who once were close to us. What strange, unexpected form might they take when they decided to reappear among us? Long after the poem was finished, I thought there was another reason for pairing the bird with my father. I felt guilty about both: my father for my not loving him enough, the bird for my not challenging my neighbours about his condition and in some way, saving him. Could I have rescued my father from the sadness of his own loneliness? If I had forgiven him for his alcoholism, could I have made his life better?"

MICHAEL CRUMMEY lives in St. John's. He has published ten books of poetry and fiction. *Little Dogs: New and Selected Poems* was published by House of Anansi in the spring of 2016.

Of "Minke Whale in Slo-mo," Crummey writes, "The yellow dory in this poem belongs to Michael Winter. He has a summer place next to mine in Western Bay. He takes the dory out on the ocean on a regular basis and when he isn't getting lost in fog, or being flipped by the swell as he rows into the beach, he is sometimes harassed by whales. He gets a surprising amount of this material on film. The thirty-second clip in question is part of a longer shot of one such encounter, slowed down and close up. Impossible to tell what's happening until that Holy Shit moment, which strikes me every time I see it. You might be able to find the clip somewhere on the Internet still."

KAYLA CZAGA lives in East Vancouver. She is the author of *For Your Safety Please Hold On* (Nightwood Editions, 2014), which won The Gerald Lampert Memorial Award and was nominated for The Governor General's Award and the Dorothy Livesay Poetry Prize, among others. Recent poems of hers are forthcoming in *PRISM international*, *Room Magazine*, *The Rusty Toque*, and *ARC Poetry Magazine*. Czaga works at "possibly the nerdiest bar in Canada," according to the *National Post*.

Of "That Great Burgundy-Upholstered Beacon of Dependability," Czaga writes, "I love where language goes wrong. How quickly a household item becomes an innuendo. I feel like these near misses are where poetry occurs most frequently for me: snags in the usual snooze-fest of language that shimmer in their wrongness. That's where the poem began, one night with my housemate Mona, an ESL teacher, telling me about teaching one nightstand vs. one-night stand. The rest of the poem tries to untangle that snag, the subtle difference between human and object. Mona's son loved a bicycle pump with an obsessive ferocity. My mom loved a van because her marriage was unsatisfying. It's easy to love an object which stays where you put it, unless a guardian is trying to yank it away and tuck you in, unless it dies in your driveway. It's hard to love a person who is walking away from you, who could die or cheat on you at any moment. It's really, really hard to aspire to love an object with another person."

MARY DALTON lives in St. John's, where she is Professor of English at Memorial University of Newfoundland. She is the author of five books of poetry, among them *Merrybegot*, *Red Ledger*, and *Hooking: A Book of Centos* (2013). A collection of Dalton's prose writings, *Edge: Essays, Reviews, Interviews*, was released by Palimpsest Press in 2015. A letterpress chapbook, *Waste Ground*, with illustrations by wood engraver Abigail Rorer, was released in June 2017 by Running the Goat Books.

Of "A Little Tin Pail," Dalton writes, "This variation on the ancient cento (a compilation of lines from one author as a form of tribute) is part of a much longer series. The poems raise questions about the nature of subjectivity, originality, quotation, tonality, musicality. Various seemingly contradictory sets of impulses are at play in the work. I came to this particular form of collage before I knew of the existence of the cento of tradition. I invented it to meet the needs of a specific piece I was working in. I then discovered that it allowed me to address a number of questions about the making of poetry. The lines that appear in 'A Little Tin Pail' are taken from the fifth lines of the following poems, in the order given: Robert Bly, 'Listening to the Köln Concert'; William Carlos Williams, 'Smell'; Michael Blumenthal, 'A Man Lost by a River'; Miguel Hernandez, 'War,' trans. Hardie St. Martin; Rainer Maria Rilke, 'Sometimes A Man Stands Up During Supper,' trans. Robert Bly; Federico García Lorca, 'Rundown Church (Ballad of the First World War),' trans. Robert Bly; Louis Simpson, 'Big Dream, Little Dream'; Rainer Maria Rilke, 'Sonnets to Orpheus VIII,' trans. Robert Bly; William Jay Smith, 'American Primitive'; Mary Oliver, 'Blue Iris'; Kerry Hardie, 'Dublin Train, Solstice'; Ezra Pound, 'Canto LXXXI'; Katha Pollitt, 'Onion'; Ann Egan, 'Lyre Blackbird'; Stanley Kunitz, 'The Portrait'; Robert Mezey, 'A Thousand Chinese Dinners'; Anna Akhmatova, 'Twenty-First. Night. Monday,' trans. Jane Kenyon; David Ignatow, 'A First on TV'; Ann Egan, 'Kind in Sounds';

Kerry Hardie, 'Le Cheval,' from 'Sunflowers'; Louis Simpson, 'American Poetry'; Robert Bly, 'Passing An Orchard By Train'; Charles Simic, 'Breasts'; Harry Martinson, 'The Earthworm,' trans. Robert Bly."

SADIQA DE MEIJER was born in Amsterdam to parents of Dutch and Kenyan-Pakistani-Afghani origins, and has lived in Canada since the age of twelve. Her poetry has been published in a range of journals, including *The Malahat Review*, *CV2*, and *Poetry Magazine*, and was awarded the CBC Poetry Prize. Her first collection, *Leaving Howe Island*, was a finalist for the Pat Lowther Memorial Award, and the Governor General's Literary Award.

De Meijer writes, "The impulse for 'Exhibit' came from a sight in a parking lot: small girls in winter coats and glittering saris, ready to celebrate Diwali. I liked the combination of the bleak weather and setting with the festive clothes and atmosphere. The poem almost wrote itself, fracturing out in a series of associations—salwar kameez and Eid, and gazes, and forms of violence. It was satisfying to use the term salwar kameez recurrently, as if, in a reversal of the shame the poem references, I could now insist on its presence in English. Later, I realized that Victor Hernández Cruz's poem, 'Puerta Rico,' in which the name Puerto Rico is repeated like an incantation, was somewhere in my mind. I've noticed, in thrift stores, that salwar kameez and saris are in a new section called 'ethnic clothing'. But as the idea of these as costume fades, there are attempts to outlaw other forms of so-called ethnic dress. That's public. Privately, acknowledging what you have tried to disown might save you. I'm intrigued by subjects that traverse that range."

BARRY DEMPSTER lives in Holland Landing, ON. Twice nominated for the Governor General's Award, Dempster is the author of fifteen collections of poetry, two volumes of short stories, two novels, and a children's book. In 2010 and 2015, he was a finalist for the Ontario Premier's Award for Excellence in the Arts. He was also nominated for the 2014 Trillium Award for his second novel, *The Outside World*. He's presently the acquisitions editor for Brick Books.

Of "Groin," Dempster writes, "A visit to the doctor's office, a sense of threatened self, a mild case of shame in having to say the word "groin" to the medical secretary—these hardly seemed like optimum conditions for a poem. But a poem was nonetheless stirring at the very hint of mortality. In fact, the poem was already planning to teach me a thing or two about the lyric impulse having no boundaries, about language and its musical intensities tuning up in the strangest places. 'Careful,' I whispered to the doctor as he donned his latex gloves, 'there's a poem in there and it hurts.'"

JERAMY DODDS grew up in Orono, ON and lives in Montreal. His first collection of poems, *Crabwise to the Hounds* (Coach House Books, 2008), was shortlisted for the Griffin Poetry Prize and won the Trillium Book Award for poetry. His most recent publications are a translation of the *Poetic Edda* (Coach House Books, 2014) and *Drakkar Noir* (Coach House Books, 2017).

Dodds writes, "'The Gift' comes from a long lineage of list poems. It has been informed by the landscape and rumours rampant throughout the Southern Ontario counties and lakefronts."

GLEN DOWNIE worked in cancer care in Vancouver for many years, and now lives in Toronto (and at www.glendownie.com). He served as Writer-in-Residence at Dalhousie University's Medical Humanities Program, and won the Toronto Book Award for his 2007 *Loyalty Management*. He has letterpress-printed two series of signed broadsides by Canadian and American poets (available through talltreepress.com). His most recent collection is *Democratic Beauties*, published by Tightrope Books.

Of "Nocturnal Visitors," Downie writes, "The pest removal vans are coming for them, because they've knocked over our compost bins once too often. Meanwhile we're spilling thousands of gallons of oil a day into the ocean. Is somebody coming for us?"

SUSAN ELMSLIE was born in Brampton, ON, and lives in Montreal. Her publications include *I, Nadja, and Other Poems* (Brick, 2006)—winner of the A.M. Klein Poetry Prize—and *Museum of Kindness* (Brick, 2017). A Hawthornden Poetry Fellow, Susan holds an MA in Canadian Literature (Western) and a PhD in English (McGill). In 2007, "Box" was selected by Parliamentary Poet Laureate John Steffler as the winner of *Arc Poetry Magazine*'s Poem of the Year contest.

Of "Box," Elmslie writes, "I was thinking about this poem for years before writing it. I'd rehearse the scene in my head, trying to figure out what it meant to me personally as well as what shape it should take as a poem, so that it might be meaningful to others. Ultimately, I wanted to dramatize, in the form of a short (box-like) poem, the sort of narrative trajectory you see in a Künstlerroman, a story of becoming an artist. I wondered if there was an equivalent literary term for a poem concerned with the poet's *prise de conscience* and burgeoning recognition of the power of words—there ought to be."

RAOUL FERNANDES lives and writes in Vancouver, with his wife and two sons. His first collection of poems, *Transmitter and Receiver* (Nightwood Editions, 2015) won the Dorothy Livesay Award and the Debut-litzer Award for Poetry in 2016 and was a finalist for the Gerald Lampert Memorial

Award and the Canadian Authors Association Award for Poetry. He has been published in numerous literary journals and anthologies.

Of "White Noise Generator," Fernandes writes, "I started writing these fragments soon after watching Amanda Todd's devastating flash-card video of her story of being intensely harassed and manipulated online and off-line before she took her life in 2012. I felt the tragedy was the result of a succession of failures of empathy, especially the ones that happen in our current online realities, and especially towards women. Failures that we all make at varying degrees in all our lives. That's where I began. I rarely write about a very raw emotional event; usually I need to sit with it for a long time before I can do anything. So there's a kind of desperation in parts of the poem. Oddly, perhaps, the first line that let me enter the poem was 'Never interrupt a girl when she is trying to draw a horse.' Her video was a powerful, heartbreaking piece of its own and matters more than my fractured attempt to come to terms with it. I think we have gained something immense from her strength and courage to share her story from the depths of that dark place. We cannot give back to her, but we can listen as hard as we can."

SAMUEL GARRIGÓ MEZA lives in Montréal. He works as a freelance gallery technician, translator, handyman, and property manager. He received a BA in Philosophy from the University of Calgary in 2005. His works have appeared in *The Capilano Review* and *dANDelion*.

Meza writes, "Each sentence was collected from a research project that involved capturing, tagging, and releasing bears for future recapture. Each sentence was taken from the research paper that resulted from each of the research projects mentioned above. Each sentence began with 'Each bear,' and each sentence that didn't was modified so that it did. For a time, I wanted to write bears and for bears to write themselves. 'Capture Recapture' appeared somewhere in the middle of my bear years. I was living alone then, in a derelict apartment building in downtown Calgary. Across the hall lived an old woman who took care of a homeless drug-addict named Happy—he spent his summers on the front lawn, shirtless, working on his 1958 VW Beetle. Three musicians lived in the basement. Upstairs was a Cameroonian man who worked at a grocery store. I loved that apartment. I painted my living room bright green and my kitchen orange. I don't know what made me so hungry for bears back then. I thought lots about ducks, too."

MICHELLE GOOD is of Cree ancestry and a member of the Battle River Cree. Prior to being accepted into UBC law at forty years of age, she worked with Indigenous people all over Canada as well as in the US. After graduating law school she worked on residential school cases for over fifteen years, operating her own firm for the last six. She has been deeply involved in the issue of residential schools since before litigation was contemplated. In 2014 she earned her Master's Degree in Fine Arts (Creative Writing) at UBC and is narrowing in on the final strokes of a novel. Her poetry has been published in the sixth edition of the anthology *Gatherings*, and in literary magazines including *West 49th* and *The Puritan*.

Good writes, "Rising from my grief at the death of my son, my only child, 'Defying Gravity' is an expression of incomprehensible loss and unlikely hope of renewal. The title is a double-entendre meant to convey the weightless, careless joy of summer rivers, both tangible and symbolic, juxtaposed against the drowning sensation of grief. It expresses my wistful desire to be the water of life again; to be the river that might deliver him back to me and me back to halcyon days. The poem started, less than two years after Jay died, as a long rambling wail; a grief-stricken keen; a modern-day grieving ritual, my heart excised and splattered on the page. I had the very good fortune of being able to workshop the poem with a wonderful group which, when everyone was finished crying, gave me solid perspectives on its strength as a poem. I took their notes and my own, sat in the sun, communed with that Boy of mine and 'River' became 'Defying Gravity.' I wanted this poem to be like a mantra—a way of going back using the sounds, sights and smells of rivers in their natural places to create a tangible connection to the best of times before time stopped. The title was divinely inspired. I didn't think if it. It just arrived. I feel Jay's hand in this poem, reaching to console and to remind that there is meaning and beauty in even the darkest times."

SUE GOYETTE lives in Halifax. She has published five poetry collections and a novel. Her latest collection, *Penelope in first person*, is forthcoming from Gaspereau Press. She's been nominated for several awards, including the 2014 Griffin Poetry Prize, and has won the CBC Literary Prize for Poetry, the Bliss Carman, the Pat Lowther, the J.M. Abraham Poetry Award, the ReLit Award, and the 2015 Lieutenant Governor of Nova Scotia Masterworks Award for her collection, *Ocean*.

Of "On Losing Their Father," Goyette writes, "I wrote this poem from the hard shore of having to parent my children through grief. I say children but, at this point, they're adults. The unexpected death of their father whittled them down to children again, and I was all they had left. I wrote so many pages in those early months, not to get to the poetry of the experience, but to pull myself through the swamp of that hard and sad time with the only thing I could rely on, my writing practice. This was one of the first poems that felt like something worthy was being addressed, that the pace grief demands had asserted itself somehow and that the poem had travelled far enough from my biography to have widened into material."

LAURIE D. GRAHAM comes from Treaty 6 territory, and she currently lives in Haldimand Treaty territory, where she is a poet, an editor, the publisher of *Brick* magazine, and a member of the advisory board for the Oskana Poetry & Poetics series. Her first book, *Rove*, was nominated for the Gerald Lampert Memorial Award, and her second book, *Settler Education*, was nominated for the Trillium Award for Poetry.

Of "Say Here, Here," Graham writes, "This bruiser jumped into the boat while I was working on an MFA in writing with the University of Guelph and living in a cheap apartment surrounded by mansions in the Forest Hill Village neighbourhood of Toronto. I had for about a week a perilously unsaved Word document open on my laptop at the kitchen table/my office, and every time I got near it I'd add another line, a few more words, another image. It was writing by accretion (which was unusual for me), big and enraged (not as unusual). I did a fair bit of pacing. Tough because the apartment was very small. That was step one. I can't recall the point at which I noticed this poem was trying to talk about property, possession, land—specifically prairie land and loss—but from early on the poem strained to be chronological (albeit with massive, unaccountable gaps) and fast like time-lapse photography. The repetition of the imperative say, by no means an original device (see Lisa Robertson's "The Weather" for a much better example), might provide an anchor through all the jumps between images, or lend rhythm or tension through repetition, or entreat the reader to form the words, to row into that place herself. Those says refuse to sit nicely though, and the lines reject the smooth break, in spite of my numerous attempts to tidy them up. This poem wants nothing to do with tidy."

JASON GURIEL lives in Toronto. He is the author of a book of essays and several poetry collections, including *Satisfying Clicking Sound* (Signal Editions, 2014). His work has appeared in such publications as *Elle*, *The Atlantic*, *The Walrus*, and *Slate*.

Of "Spineless Sonnet," Guriel writes, "I like poems that plunder what Eliot calls 'the unexplored resources of the unpoetical.' I don't know if a sock puppet is 'unpoetical,' but I'm not sure I've ever seen one in a sonnet. Anyway, there's a perverse thrill in writing about such a seemingly trivial thing in such a seemingly serious form."

PHIL HALL lives near Perth, ON. His most recent books are *Guthrie Clothing: The Poetry of Phil Hall—A Selected Collage* (Wilfrid Laurier University Press, 2015), and *Conjugation* (BookThug, 2016). He has won numerous awards, and been writer-in-residence at many universities and colleges. In 2010, he established The Page Lectures at Queen's University in Kingston.

Hall writes, "There is power in saying who did what to whom. 'Fletched' means to have feathers attached to the shafts of arrows. This is a poem concerning sexual child abuse and revision, or how soul murder bends the bow. It is like a novel, in that a life is told in cinematic flashes with big gaps that include rumination, and bathos. I mean these long one-line stanzas and their ruthless aim to be collective and humane. *Forget Magazine* published the poem on Canada Day, and put a photo of a large white flag with it!"

STEVEN HEIGHTON lives in Kingston, ON. His most recent poetry collection, *The Waking Comes Late*, won the 2016 Governor General's Award for Poetry and was a finalist for the Raymond Souster Award. His poems have appeared in *London Review of Books, Poetry, Agni, Best American Poetry, London Magazine, TLR, The Walrus*, and five editions of *Best Canadian Poetry in English*. He also writes reviews for the *NYTBR* and publishes fiction, most recently the novel *The Nightingale Won't Let You Sleep*.

Heighton writes, "'Some Other Just Ones' is a response to Jorge Luis Borges's poem 'The Just' ('*El Justo*'). The italicized first and last lines that frame my poem are translated from the Spanish of Borges's original; the rest is my own simple litany or catalogue of those people who, in small ways, redeem the day. I don't usually write 'from life,' not without radical transformation, but, in this case, most of my lines are based on real people, people living here in Kingston. I don't usually write list-poems, either, because when I do I tend to get sloppy, plausibly fluent, lazily capacious—all dangers endemic to the form. But I loved the Borges original and I'd been writing some harsh judgmental poems and I craved a furlough from indignation. I wanted to sing about my neighbours and the people I know—even the ones I dislike in some ways, since they too are saviours of something. In the same way that it's easier to maintain grievance than gratitude, it seems easier for most poets to write 'negative' stuff (sad, angry, grieving) than 'positive.' Certainly that's been true in my own case. But my experience of writing, publishing, and performing 'Some Other just Ones' has been so, yes, positive that I know I'll try writing this way again."

JASON HEROUX lives in Kingston, ON and published *Hard Work Cheering Up Sad Machines* in the spring of 2016 with Mansfield Press. He is the author of *Memoirs of an Alias* (2004), *Emergency Hallelujah* (2008), *Good Evening, Central Laundromat* (2010), *Natural Capital* (2012) and *We Wish You a Happy Killday* (2014). His work has appeared in magazines and journals in Canada, the U.S., Belgium, France, and Italy and has been translated into French, Italian, and Arabic.

Of "Allowance," Heroux writes, "I finished reading Alfred Starr Hamilton's posthumous collection *A Dark Dreambox of Another Kind* (The Song Cave, 2013) and was struck by his ability to blend child-like wonder with adult complexities. I tried to write 'Allowance' in that same spirit. The poem started off as a stand-alone piece but eventually became part of a sequence titled The Vending Machine of Earthly Delights. I play with the title 'Allowance' as meaning both the allowance our parents give use as children, as well as the allowance to do something we're not usually permitted to do. The poem asks: how much of what we do is done because it's expected of us? Not just as children living under our parents' roof, but as citizens living under society's roof, and ultimately as organisms living under the roof of an ecosystem. How do we spend the life we're allowed to live? One of the things I like most about the poem is the speaker's neutral tone, as if he's just describing the facts of life. You take the good. You take the bad. You take them both and then eventually give everything back."

SEAN HOWARD lives in the lobster-fishing village of Main-à-Dieu, Cape Breton. The author of *Local Calls* (Cape Breton University Press, 2009), *Incitements* (Gaspereau Press, 2011), and *The Photographer's Last Picture* (Gaspereau Press, 2016), his poetry has been widely published in Canada, the US, UK, and elsewhere. Sean is adjunct professor of political science at Cape Breton University, researching nuclear disarmament, the political history of twentieth-century physics, and the politics and culture of war commemoration.

Howard writes, "Since 2006, I have been working on a project to take 'shadowgraphs'—or *poetic X-rays*—of selected Nobel Physics lectures. Using an adaptation of William Burroughs' Dada-inspired 'cut-up' method, my aim is to expose and examine hidden and unsuspected connections, contradictions, and even pathologies beneath the polished, settled surface of the prose. 'Shadowgraph 52' is, I think, one of my most successful experiments so far."

HELEN HUMPHREYS lives in Kingston, ON, where she is also the city's poet laureate. Humphreys is the award-winning author of four books of poetry, seven novels, and three works of creative non-fiction. Her most recent works are *The Evening Chorus* (HarperCollins, 2015) and *The River* (ECW Press, 2015).

Of "Auden's House," Humphreys writes, "When I was a young writer, W.H. Auden was the poet I most admired. Years later, I had the chance to visit his house in Kirchstetten, Austria. In between my young self and the visit to the great poet's house, I had become disillusioned—with poetry, and with myself.

But getting a glimpse of the man Auden was, as I stood in his study at the top of his house, somehow gave me permission to argue with the self I had been when I first became a poet—the self I suddenly realized I no longer was."

MAUREEN HYNES lives in Toronto. Her book, *Rough Skin*, won the League of Canadian Poets' Gerald Lampert Award for best first book of poetry by a Canadian. Her fourth book of poetry, *The Poison Colour*, was shortlisted for both the League's Raymond Souster and Pat Lowther Awards in 2017. Her work has been included in over 20 anthologies, and twice longlisted for the CBC Canada Reads poetry contest. Maureen is poetry editor for *Our Times* magazine. (maureenhynes.com)

Hynes writes, "'The Last Cigarette' is a both a marker and an invocation as I renounced an addiction. I'd planned to quit smoking before I took a kayaking trip off Haida Gwaii (Queen Charlotte Islands), and I'd also immersed myself in the art, culture, and legends of the Haida. Just before the kayaking trip, I drove myself up to Massett for a ceremonial moment in the north island to smoke the last few cigarettes in my pack. If I could paint the moment, it would be in shades of grey. I hope the poem captures those greys, my fear and panic and deluded clinging to the sensuality of smoking, and my plea to all the Haida spirits who'd given and endured so much—and the bracing coldness of the surf to restore health and sanity."

SALLY ITO was born in Alberta and resides in Winnipeg with her husband and two children. Her latest book is the collaboratively authored and translated children's poetry book, *Are You an Echo: The Lost Poetry of Misuzu Kaneko*. Ito's last poetry book, *Alert to Glory*, was published in 2011.

Of "Idle," Ito writes, "I wrote this poem thinking about 'idleness' as a state-of-mind experienced in the church pew. To sit through a weekly church service is a spiritual discipline that, while seemingly boring, actually serves to bring one in alignment with oneself, one's God, and one's faith community. 'Idleness' is also that gestational state often associated with creativity where the artist appears to be doing nothing, but is actually 'awaiting' inspiration, as it were. Sometimes we need to be 'put' into that space before anything arises from out of it."

AMANDA JERNIGAN was born in southern Ontario. As an adult she has lived in Ontario, New Brunswick, and Newfoundland. She is the author of two books of poetry, *Groundwork* and *All the Daylight Hours*; of the prose book *Living in the Orchard: The Poetry of Peter Sanger*; and of the libretto for *Years, Months, and Days*, by Colin Labadie. She edited *The Essential Richard Outram* and co-edited *Earth and Heaven: An Anthology of Myth Poetry*.

Jernigan writes, "In Ovid's *Metamorphoses*, Io, daughter of the river god Inachus, is raped by Zeus, who then transforms her into a white heifer—an unsuccessful attempt to hide his infidelity from his vengeful wife. Unrecognizable to her family, Io wanders the earth in this form—first captive to Argus the hundred-eyed, Hera's appointed jailer; then tormented by a Fury—until at length, beside the river Nile, she regains her natural shape. In some accounts Io's tormentor is a gadfly, but in A.D. Melville's translation of the *Metamorphoses*, the tormentor is a Fury set 'Before her... eyes and in her mind': a demon, like the marks of trauma, as much internal as external. 'Io' is one in a series of *Metamorphoses* poems—each ten lines long, in loosely-rhyming couplets—that I began writing after my first son's birth. They were poems that I could work on in my head as I was nursing a baby or pulling a wagon: formal exercises in repetition-and-variation. But at the same time, they were meditations on change, coming out of a time of life in which metamorphosis is everywhere apparent. The register of these poems is mythological, but the impetus is personal: this is true of the series as a whole, and also of the individual poems with their dramatis personae in whose stories I have seen my own both told and changed. 'Io' is for my sister."

MICHAEL JOHNSON was born and raised in Bella Coola, BC. He's the author of *How to Be Eaten by a Lion* (Nightwood Editions, 2016), and his work has appeared widely in literary journals including *The Fiddlehead, Shenandoah, Mid-American Review, The Malahat Review, The Southern Review,* and in the *Best American* and *Best Canadian Poetry* anthologies. He lives with his family in Penticton, BC, and works at a local winery.

Of "The Church of Steel," Johnson writes, "My dad owns a milling machine from a World War II battleship. Patented in 1908. I've waited years to tell that. To tell how the belt chugged along like it might never die. How the bits gnawed away whatever I wanted to cut—how metal was a language I'd been taught since my toddling. Dad used to let me hold things, sometimes even try the taste of it all. So many scars, so much time pounding the panels of cars, torquing bolts—it hit me one day: I'd long lived in the church of steel. I had been writing poems with "church" titles—"The Church of My Mother's Hands," "The Church of Rot," "The Church of Thorn and Thicket"... —so I started with a title that intrigued me and just the word "knurl." Grit in the oyster of my mouth. I couldn't let it go. I asked my dad what that trick with the lathe was called, and the width of the cut, and what it was all made of. And much like the projects of my growing up, I honed and trimmed and polished what felt like praise."

KHÂSHA/Stephen Reid writes, "I was born in 1979 at Whitehorse Hospital to Michael Reid and Frances Lucier. On my mother's side I was raised up around Whitehorse. On my father's side I was raised up around Bella Bella. Took me a while to learn how to read, but I suppose I got it figured out now. I come from a large family, maybe that's why I now have my own large family. I work at Elijah Smith School as a Dän k'è language teacher."

Of "Bush Indian," Khâsha writes, "I still enjoy this poem, a friend of five years, maybe. Even today, this poem can teach me, remind me of my role as a younger 'Dan' person. The children are taken care of and taught. The adults are working for the people. The young adults should not speak too much; that is for the older ones. The older ones are giving back all their teachings. This is how I understand it at least. It took everything in me to write this poem. There is so much to do on our journey to express the ancestors inside of us. Though I enjoyed writing it, I needed to be amongst my people even more so. 'So I get busy because what the hell are words.' Our identity lives on the land, our identity is from our people."

SONNET L'ABBÉ, PhD, was born in Toronto and lives on Vancouver Island. She is the author of *A Strange Relief* and *Killarnoe*, and was the 2014 guest editor of *Best Canadian Poetry*. Her chapbook of plant-human poems, *Anima Canadensis*, was published by Junction Books in 2016. In her latest collection, *Sonnet's Shakespeare*, (McClelland and Stewart, 2018), L'Abbé "writes over" all 154 of Shakespeare's sonnets. Poems from *Sonnet's Shakespeare* appear in Best American Experimental Writing 2016. L'Abbé is a professor of Creative Writing and English at Vancouver Island University.

Of "The Trees Have Loved Us All Along," L'Abbe writes, "My obsession for the past three years has been to feel out why we use plant metaphors to talk about three things: language (root words), our nervous and neurological systems (dendrites, stem cells and brain stems, seminal ideas), and organizational structures (bank branches, decision trees). Spiritual growth as a biological something? Joy as a kind of photosynthesis? Sometimes my pursuit seems a little crazy, like hunting for a cure to a sickness we haven't discovered yet. I wonder, why do I care so much about how we are like plants? Then I go out and notice a tree. I am struck again by something central, something elemental and balanced. My body relaxes, my breath slows. There is movement at the centre of rings of pith and through the spinal column. That trunk there—is alive. My mindbody tries to organize that perception into words. Sex is somewhere at the heart of it."

BEN LADOUCEUR is a writer living in Ottawa. His first collection of poems, *Otter* (Coach House Books), was selected as a best book of 2015 by the *National Post*, nominated for a 2016 Lambda Literary Award, and awarded the 2016 Gerald Lampert Memorial Award for best debut poetry collection in Canada. He recently completed a three-month-long residency at the Al Purdy A-Frame in Ameliasburgh, ON.

Of "I Am in Love with Your Brother," Ladouceur writes, "The title came first, and the entire poem is more or less a frame for it. It's an awkward confession to make, and the poem bolsters that awkwardness by taking the form of a wedding speech. I've seen it happen at more than one wedding: a character from the groom's distant past stands to make a speech and addresses the newlywed sentimentally, but the sentiment feels outdated. The groom is now a different man. In this poem, the speaker takes the opportunity to tell a truth, perhaps struggling to imagine that he'll ever speak to 'Richie' again."

FIONA TINWEI LAM immigrated to Vancouver from Scotland at the age of four. She has authored *Intimate Distances* (Nightwood, 2002: City of Vancouver Book Prize Finalist), *Enter the Chrysanthemum* (Caitlin, 2009) and the children's book, *The Rainbow Rocket* (Oolichan, 2013). She edited *The Bright Well: Contemporary Canadian Poems on Facing Cancer* (Leaf, 2011). Her poetry videos have been screened internationally. She teaches at Simon Fraser University's Continuing Studies. fionalam.net

Of "Aquarium," Lam writes, "When my son was an infant and toddler, I wrote a sequence of poems set in ordinary places that detailed the journey into single parenthood. (Many of these poems were included in *Enter the Chrysanthemum*.) There can be precise and lucid moments where the symbolic potential within even the most mundane of activities is revealed. This poem about loss juxtaposes tone and style to both mirror and frame its content. The poem moves from inside to outside, ideal to real, protected to exposed, whole to incomplete, with the middle stanza bridging the two poles. The intensity and intimacy of the poem are linked to its apparent simplicity."

SANDRA LAMBERT was born in Lachine, QC, and lives in Toronto. She works as a fundraiser for a children's rehabilitation hospital, and paints in the off hours. Her work has been published in *Arc Poetry Magazine*, *CV2*, and *The New Quarterly*. A series of her poems was shortlisted for the CBC Literary Awards in 2005.

Of "Our Lady of Rue Ste Marie," Lambert writes "I grew up on Ste Marie Avenue, a tiny cul de sac in the old French Canadian village of Dorval on the shores of Lac St. Louis, near Lachine, Québec. The title refers to a modernist metal statue, which stands in the backyard of a neighbour's house in Dorval.

The statue may or may not represent the Virgin Mary—it stands on private property, and there is no plaque. The area was a bird sanctuary when my parents first moved there in the 1950s to escape the dirt and poverty of Verdun. Old Dorval is steeped in the history and romance of Québec. In 1665, the village was a pallisaded mission known as Gentilly and later La Présentation (referring to the Presentation of the Holy Virgin). In writing the poem, I was inspired by my childhood memories of Québec as well as Amy Gerstler's poem, *Modern Madonnas*, Diane Schoemperlen's novel, *Our Lady of the Lost and Found*, and Greek, Sumerian, and Tibetan hymns and stories of the Goddess."

M. TRAVIS LANE lives in Fredericton, NB. She received her BA from Vassar College and her M. and PhD from Cornell University, taught briefly at Cornell and at the University of New Brunswick, and has been an honorary Research Associate with the English department at UNB for many years. She is a member of the Voice of Women for Peace and a Raging Granny. She has published seventeen books of poetry and was shortlisted for the Governor General's Award in 2015, and received the Lieutenant Governor's Award for Excellence in the Literary Arts in 2017. Her poem "Bird Count" appeared in her collection *Crossover* in 2015.

Lane writes, "In Fredericton we take nature seriously, especially birds. The Fredericton Christmas Bird Count is a significant enterprise in which, however, I have never participated, partly due to my dislike of standing about in the snow, partly because I cannot maintain a bird feeder in winter, and partly, too, because by the time I can see a bird it has flown away. (People on the edge of town feed bears as well as birds at their feeders, but as yet Fredericton has not an annual Bear Count—Easter would be the best time for that!) What I like most about birds is their character, their varying personalities, their exuberance, the intensity of their being whatever it is they are being. 'Bird Count' is not a naturalist's poem. Read it as an unnaturalist's poem. Frivolous. As some Victorian child is reputed (by Beerbohm) to have addressed the often frivolous (at tea parties) poet Matthew Arnold, 'Oh Uncle Arnold, why can you not be wholly serious?'"

EVELYN LAU is the Vancouver author of twelve books, including seven volumes of poetry. Her work has received the Milton Crown Award, the Pat Lowther Award, a National Magazine Award, and a Governor-General's Award nomination. Evelyn served as 2011-2014 Poet Laureate for the City of Vancouver. Her most recent collection, *Tumour*, was released by Oolichan Books in 2016.

Lau writes, "I think of 'Grandmother' as a sort of companion piece to

'Grandfather,' an earlier poem of mine, which also appeared in *Ricepaper*. In 'Grandfather,' his wife is depicted harshly and without sentiment. My grandmother was a tyrannical woman, legendary for her epic rages. She was also the mother of twelve children—one son, eleven daughters—a responsibility I can't begin to imagine. Although we hadn't seen each other for many years, when she died I felt the urge to write a poem that tried to be sympathetic to who she was, to recall the warmth she showed me as a child, and to end on a positive note that spanned the generations."

RACHEL LEBOWITZ lives in Halifax, NS, where she coordinates tutoring programs at her community library. Her first book, *Hannus* (Pedlar Press, 2006), was shortlisted for the 2007 Roderick Haig-Brown Regional BC Book Prize and the Edna Staebler Award for Creative Non-Fiction. Her other books are the children's picture book *Anything But Hank!* (Biblioasis, 2008) and *Cottonopolis* (Pedlar Press, 2013). Her latest book, *The Year of No Summer*, is forthcoming from Biblioasis in 2018.

Of "*from* Cottonopolis," Lebowitz writes "These poems are from a book sequence of prose-and-found poems about the Industrial Revolution, specifically the links between the cotton industry in Lancashire and slavery. I've combed many history books for arresting images: vultures resting on rusted guns at the British slave fort Cape Coast Castle, slaves' bodies shining with palm oil (to make them appear healthier than they were so they could be sold), dying slave ship sailors huddled in sugar casks, buyers moving slaves' fingers back and forth to see how well they'll pick cotton—these are poems already! I bring them here, add new details, toss in some harsh words here, some hibiscus there. The art of it is important to me but mostly it is my hope that through this, the stories will still be heard."

DENNIS LEE was born in Toronto, where he still lives. He has published some forty books, most recently *Melvis and Elvis* (2015) and *Heart Residence: Collected Poems 1967-2017* (2017). He co-founded House of Anansi Press in 1967, wrote the song lyrics for Jim Henson's *Fraggle Rock*, and served as Toronto's first Poet Laureate. As a resident artist at Soulpepper Theatre Company, he initiated the *Lost Songs of Toronto* cabaret, 2012-2014.

Lee writes, "'Slipaway' belongs with the poems of *Un* (2003) and *Yesno* (2007). But there, the degradation of the planet was handled in a language that often fractured under the pressure of the unthinkable. For whatever reason, more recent pieces like 'Slipaway' have emerged in something like recognizable English."

SHELLEY A. LEEDAHL was born and raised in Saskatchewan and now lives in Ladysmith, BC. She works in multiple genres and is the author of a dozen books, including *The Moon Watched it All* (Red Deer Press, 2017); *I Wasn't Always Like This* (Signature Editions, 2014); *Listen, Honey* (DC Books, 2012); *Wretched Beast* (BuschekBooks, 2011); and *The House of the Easily Amused* (Oolichan Books, 2008). She writes book reviews and freelances for diverse markets.

Of "Single Pansy Among the Stones," Leedahl writes "In 2011-2012 I lived tri-provincially: on the edge of a rural Saskatchewan village (where rolling up one's sleeves and growing a sizeable garden was well-respected, and coyotes sang me to sleep); in frenetic innercity Edmonton (where sirens pierced the air day and night, but the art scene was exceptional); and in gorgeous, coastal Sechelt, BC (where the waves mesmerized, and a pod of orcas cavorted before my eyes). Each of these disparate landscapes held specific charms, but most inspiring—perhaps because it was most foreign to me—was my time spent in the rented oceanfront home in Sechelt. Everything was new— from my view of seals, sailboats and bald eagles to the mild climate; from the lush, old-growth forests to my leisure activities, which included throwing crab traps. I decided to write a series of 25-word poems that might capture—like an enthusiastic tourist's quick-fire snapshots—the almost child-like awe I was experiencing in this new landscape. I wrote about tugboats and jellyfish and Himalayan blackberries. And I wrote about a single pansy, among stones. These minimalistic pieces varied greatly from my usual, almost-conversational poetic style. In keeping with all the other "freshness" of the Sunshine Coast experience, perhaps I subconsciously felt I also needed to write in a different form. Regardless, it was good fun. I existed in a state of enchantment for the ten months I resided in Sechelt. Perhaps one day I'll permanently return."

KIRYA MARCHAND was born in Montréal where she currently works as an exotic veterinary assistant and zoo educator. She studied literature and environmental sciences at McGill University and was awarded the Lionel Shapiro Award for Creative Writing (2013). In 2016, she began pursuing post-graduate studies in animal welfare with the University of Edinburgh. Her poetry has previously appeared in *GRAIN*, *The Antigonish Review*, and *PRISM*.

Marchand writes, "This poem represents an exploration of its own textuality. Silly, self-reflexive, and fun to say out loud, 'Hamlet' is a response to a question posed by James McLaverty and put forward again by Jerome McGann in his work, *The Textual Condition: 'If the Mona Lisa is hanging in the Louvre in Paris, where is Hamlet?'* The reader is hence invited to follow a trail of clues that leads from Shakespeare's studio all the way to the pocketbooks of modern day Beijing, all in pursuit of the melancholic prince. By the end, the reader should be more aware of both Hamlet's odd elusiveness and ubiquity, and of the role we ourselves play in his ongoing history."

DAVE MARGOSHES lives on a farm west of Saskatoon with his partner, poet-essayist-fiction writer Dee Hobsbawn-Smith. He has published five poetry collections. The most recent, *Dimensions of an Orchard*, won the Poetry Prize at the 2010 Saskatchewan Book Awards. His poems have won a number of other awards, including the inaugural Stephen Leacock Prize for Poetry, and have appeared widely in magazines and anthologies. A new collection, *A Calendar of Reckoning*, is forthcoming.

Margoshes writes, "I frequently mine my own life for poems, as most poets do. Often the 'autobiography' is as much fiction as it is fact. 'The Chicken Coop' is as close to real autobiography as any of my poems—it's an enduring part of the mythology of my family, but there really was a converted chicken coop, a lost house, an old farm, the glass of port in my father's hand, his regret. On the other hand, I was an infant when we lived in the coop, so the poem is based on family lore, not true memory."

SADIE MCCARNEY grew up in small-town Nova Scotia, but lives in Charlottetown, PEI. Her work has appeared in *The Puritan*, *The Malahat Review*, *Prairie Fire*, *Room*, *Grain*, and *Plenitude*, among other places. She is currently at work on a novel in verse.

McCarney writes, "'Steeltown Songs' is a fiction, but it came to me by way of two real places: the gritty little collection of mostly-failed industrial towns called Pictou County, NS (where I grew up), and the heartache of a series of entirely hopeless childhood crushes. I did most of the real writing work when I was sixteen and seventeen, but the poem had no real form then and spoke in a very distant and impersonal third-person voice. Still, I found myself drawn to the nameless lapsed-tomboy character who would later become my narrator. The day of my grade twelve prom, instead of spending hours getting my hair done for the dance, I brought a very early and incomplete draft of 'Steeltown Songs' to a poetry workshop with George Elliott Clarke. I very nervously read my fragments of poetry aloud at top speed, and everyone at the workshop encouraged me to keep working on it. But it was also hinted gently (and mercifully) that the poem wasn't quite there yet. The intervening five or six years have been mostly editing, but the process has taught me something important: never give up on a character. Never give up on a poem."

DAVID MCGIMPSEY was born in Montreal and continues to live and work there. He is the author of six collections of poetry including, most recently,

Asbestos Heights (Coach House Books), winner of the A.M. Klein Award for Poetry. His previous collection of poetry, *Li'l Bastard*, which contains "What was that poem?", was nominated for the Governor General's Award. David McGimpsey is also the author of the short fiction collection *Certifiable* and the award-winning critical study *Imagining Baseball: America's Pastime and Popular Culture*. Named by the CBC as one of the "Top Ten English language poets in Canada," David is also a food and travel writer who regularly contributes to EnRoute magazine. A PhD in American Literature, David McGimpsey teaches in the English Department of Concordia University in Montreal.

Of "What was that poem?", McGimpsey writes, "My mother, Mary Macdonald McGimpsey, knew the lines to many, many poems and songs. She attended Montreal High School in the 1930s and reciting poems was a core part of her—as she would amusingly say—'Victorian education.' She lived with the great spirit of the working class who sought education not just to fit one's self into a career but to better one's self by enjoying the good things in life. She was as comfortable listening to the opera as she was listening to a ballgame. My poem tries to commemorate her spirit and tries to do so with manners I am certain she was proud of."

DON MCKAY resides in St. John's, NL, having over time lived in many regions of the country. He has published twelve books of poetry (including a collected poems called *Angular Unconformity*) many of which have been recognized with awards such as the Governor General's Award and the Griffin Prize. He has also written essays in the genre now known as ecopoetics.

Of "Sleeping with the River," McKay writes, "A while back I spent the winter months living in the Haig-Brown House in Campbell River, BC, as writer-in-residence, with the Campbell flowing full tilt past the bedroom. As a sometime insomniac, I have the usual set of trick and technique for inducing sleep (the warm milk, the skullcap, the Valerian, the single malt, the heavy drugs). But I soon discovered that, what with the rains running through their scales and exercises and the river pouring out its blendered Berlitz, the affliction had thrown itself into reverse. I'd become a somniac. One of the many blessings of that remarkable place and time."

JACOB MCARTHUR MOONEY was born in Nova Scotia and lives in Toronto. He edited the 2015 edition of *Best Canadian Poetry in English*. His books include *Don't Be Interesting* (McClelland & Stewart, 2017) and the Dylan Thomas Prize finalist, *Folk* (M&S, 2011).

Mooney writes, "'The Fever Dreamer' is a performance poem. That is to say: when it was rumbling about in my head, before the first draft, I conceived of it as something I wanted to read out to an audience more than I wanted people to read to themselves. So as a written instrument, it is an attempted blueprint for its ideal performance. This is a pretty draconian use of prosody, and I apologize for being so stubborn a poet. As a poem, it carries with it the standard fears of historical work (getting the history of Baden Powell and his post-WWI dark period right, without burdening the text with a parade of google-prompts), but my chief interest here is sonic, not historical. I hope I get the details right, but it's really the song prompt that I care about: the theme and variation of the music. As such, I owe borrower's debts to both Rick Moody for his short story 'Boys' and Paul Vermeersch for his poem 'Ape.'"

CARA-LYN MORGAN lives and works in the Toronto area but hails a bit from the prairies and a bit further West. Her first collection of poems, *What Became My Grieving Ceremony* (Thistledown Press Ltd, 2014) won the Fred Cogswell Award for Excellence in Poetry in 2015. Her work has appeared in a number of literary presses across Canada and her second collection of poems, *Cartograph*, is set for release by Thistledown Press in the fall. Her work centres strongly around her cultural and ancestral histories, seeking a balance between the histories of her Métis mother and Caribbean-Canadian father.

Of "mîscacakânis," Morgan writes, "This poem is about reconnecting with the ancestral instinct, the ghost bones, and the places in the earth where the old family has always walked. It is about relearning the joy of space and distance; unfamiliar to those of us who have always lived surrounded in the concrete and shade of cities. My body always knows when it is back on the prairies, there is a lightening in my shoulders and my feet seem to soften. When my baby niece came to Watrous from Toronto, she seemed to feel this loosening even though she had never been to Saskatchewan before. She ran ahead of us, screaming joyfully with her hands flung up above her head. In that moment, I realized that the span of prairie is not a thing that can be described or learned; it is a nesting in the chest, a way of breathing. It is something that our oldest bones understand. This is also a poem about the sharing of stories, the rooting back to the familial voices, and the act of coming home. It was written in couplets not only to echo the pairing of the speaker and the child she is observing, but also to create expanse on the page using long lines and a lot of white space. The poem is meant to be visually wide as well as visceral, through the use of adjectives and sensory language, to loosely echo the stretch of the prairie horizon, its sharp edge and widest skies."

A.F. MORITZ lives in Toronto; his most recent book is *Sequence* (House of Anansi Press, 2015). *The New Measures* (2012) received the Raymond Souster Award of the League of Canadian Poets and was a Governor General's Award finalist, and his 2008 collection, *The Sentinel*, was awarded the Griffin

Poetry Prize and the Bess Hokin Prize of Poetry magazine. In 2015 Princeton University Press republished his 1986 book, *The Tradition*.

Of "The Clock," Moritz writes, "Maybe this poem is generated not only by its own subject but by Poe, his keen prophetic grasp of so much of modernity under the image and experience of hyperaesthesia. Maybe a painfully fascinated awareness of the commonest things, those most in the background, things scarcely seen or heard—things even unseen and unheard because we only fear or imagine they may exist—until, suddenly, they emerge as thunder, preoccupation, obsession, insomnia, paranoia... maybe this has always been part of humans. But it's certainly part of today. We fear to hear, to sense, the heart's beating and the pulse, and this fear is exaggerated by—does it perhaps originate from?—the ticking of the clock. The blood: the clock— that similar, parallel rhythm we've created to emphasize the fewness of the shortness of our breaths and days. To assert, even if it does not really exist, an external mechanical dimension to reality, not even 'opposed to' what we feel as ourselves, but simply unrelated to it in any way. Irrelevant, and entirely encompassing, overwhelming, dominant. The premature burial. The original monstrous and invulnerable alien. There is the fact that even rest is a torrent. But, then, the poem's end, as it contends to be what encloses and lies at the centre, glimpses that the torrent is rest. The storm, the disaster, the being-dragged-along, inheres in the subsequent, and the former, rest. Poe."

SHANE NEILSON is a poet, physician, and critic from New Brunswick. His fourth book of poems, *Dysphoria*, was released with the Porcupine's Quill in spring 2017. Shane was shortlisted for the Trillium Poetry Prize in 2010 and he won the Robin Blaser Award from *The Capilano Review* in 2015. His work has twice appeared in the *Best Canadian Poetry* series.

Of "My daughter imitates A.Y. Jackson's 'Road to Baie St. Paul," Neilson writes, "About a year after my daughter and son were seriously ill, but somewhat on the way to recovery, my daughter, Zee, came home from school with a painting. As part of a grade eight art class, she imitated the A.Y. Jackson painting mentioned in the poem's title. After handing the portrait to me, she asked, 'What do you think, Daddy?' I'm sure I praised her, but my reaction is subsumed in the more serious reaction that is the poem I wrote about an hour after she asked me that originating question. In her painting, I saw a speck of a man hurtling home on a horse and carriage, desperate to find his family intact. The man had a sick daughter, sick son, and a heart as vacant as the depicted landscape was violent. The horseman saw angels, and he knew he had to hurry. The place was too beautiful for him not to be worried. The man in the painting—he wrote my poem. When I learned the bargain fathers and mothers make with life, that it is fleeting, that there is no guarantee the things we love will stay, but that we are yet impotently alive to mark their passing, I reached for several texts to assist with the absorption of this truth of impermanence. One of them is William James, who appeared to me as one of the angels who said, 'The beautiful polices the most solemn passions.' I worked on that poem until it was as solemn as I could make it sound, to follow James' advice, to make the poem grieve."

HOA NGUYEN was born in the Mekong Delta, raised in the Washington, DC area, and lives in Toronto. From Wave Books, her poetry collections include *As Long As Trees Last*, *Red Juice: Poems 1998-2008*, and *Violet Energy Ingots*, nominated for a 2017 Griffin Prize for poetry. She teaches poetics at Ryerson University, for Miami University's low residency MFA program, for the Milton Avery School for Fine Arts at Bard College, and in a long-running, private workshop.

Nguyen writes, "The title of the poem 'A Thousand Times You Lose Your Treasure' is also the working title of a series in-progress, a verse meditation on a convulsive era in Vietnam. In this poem as in others in the series, I'm presenting and reimagining personal, historical, and familial perspectives."

DAVID O'MEARA lives in Ottawa. He is the author of four poetry collections, most recently *A Pretty Sight* (Coach House Press).

Of "Background Noise," O'Meara writes, "Whether it's war or neurosis, one has to engage with something in order to defeat it. But any deep engagement reveals complexity. This poem originates in superficial irritation and dilates obsessively toward discoveries of 'cosmic microwave background radiation,' evidence of the Big Bang. I have loosely referenced the 'Holmdel Horn Antenna' (look it up on Wikipedia; it's pretty cool) and the experiments done at Bell Labs in the 1950s."

MICHAEL ONDAATJE was born in Colombo, Sri Lanka, and lives in Toronto. He is the author of six novels, a memoir, a nonfiction book on film, and over a dozen books of poetry. *The English Patient* won the Booker Prize; *Anil's Ghost* won the *Irish Times* International Fiction Prize, the Giller Prize, and the Prix Médicis.

'Bruise' references Paul Vermeersch's poem 'Lost Things,' from his 2010 collection *The Reinvention of the Human Hand* (McClelland & Stewart, 2010).

P.K. PAGE was born in England and moved to Canada when she was three, subsequently living in most regions of the country. Page was the author of more than a dozen books, including poetry, a novel, short stories, essays, and books for children. Awarded a Governor General's Award for Poetry (*The Metal and the Flower*) in 1954, Page was also on the shortlist for the Griffin Poetry Prize (*Planet Earth*) in 2003 and awarded the BC Lieutenant Governor's Award for Literary excellence in 2004. P.K. Page died in January 2010. Her 2009 collection, *Coal and Roses* (Porcupine's Quill), was posthumously nominated for the 2010 Griffin Poetry Prize.

Of "Coal and Roses," Page wrote, "I have for some years been in love with the glosa form. One day a friend sent me the Akhmatova three-stanza poem, 'Everything is plundered…' And I wondered if I could write a triple glosa, moving from the worldly (grim) through nature to the sublime."

ELISE PARTRIDGE was born in the United States and spent her adult years in Canada. She was a finalist for the BC Book Prize and the Gerald Lampert Award and won the Canadian Authors Association Poetry Award. Partridge's work has been anthologized in Canada, the US, Ireland, and the UK. Her third and final collection, *The Exiles' Gallery* (House of Anansi) was published in 2015. She died in February of 2015.

Of "Two Cowboys," Partridge wrote, "While walking in downtown Vancouver one day, I caught a glimpse of a man and child, looking like father and son, dressed identically and hurrying along, the father scowling and the boy struggling to keep up. I began this poem after the image kept returning to me over subsequent months."

RUTH ROACH PIERSON lives in Toronto. She has published four poetry collections: *Where No Window Was* (BuschekBooks, 2002), *Aide-Mémoire* (BuschekBooks, 2007), finalist for the 2008 Governor General's Award for Poetry, *CONTRARY* (Tightrope, 2011), and *Realignment* (Palimpsest Press, 2015). She has also edited the anthology *I Found It at the Movies* (Guernica Editions, 2014) and published two chapbooks: *Aperture* (Rufus Books, 2014), inspired by the photography of Josef Sudek, and *Untranslatable Thought*, a collection of centos. *Till I Caught Myself* will be published by Seraphim Editions in the fall of 2017.

Of "Equipoise," Pierson writes, "This poem was inspired by a reunion with a friend I've known since my student days at the University of Washington—Valerie Bystrom, to whom, as well as to our now deceased mutual friend Diane Middlebrook, I am deeply indebted. To fulfill the elective then required by the M.A. programme in history, the two of them recommended Theodore Roethke's twentieth-century poetry course which, at their prompting, I took in 1962. Back in Seattle in the summer of 2010, after visiting the Elliott Bay Bookstore together, where I bought a copy of Fanny Howe's *The Wedding Dress: Meditations on Word and Life*, Valerie and I found a cafe on Capitol Hill and, over lunch, she told me about reaching a stage in her life when she just wants 'to float' and also about saving herself from drowning when a young girl by floating. Later, reflecting on our conversation and observing a hawk overhead, I realized how different our approaches to life now are and perhaps have always been."

MEDRIE PURDHAM teaches at the University of Regina and was the City of Regina's Writer of the Year in 2015-2016. She has published poetry in journals across the country, has broadcast a suite of poems on the former CBC radio program Sound XChange, and has twice been anthologized in *Best Canadian Poetry in English*.

Of "How the Starling Came to America: a glosa for P.K. Page," Purdham writes, "The poetry of P.K. Page is in some ways its own aviary, showing Page's delight in the creatures of the air and also her ambivalent interest in the ways in which we collect, classify and name them. It was also Page who popularized the glosa—an old Spanish form—in contemporary Canadian poetry. The glosa requires the poet to use four lines from another poet's work as an epigraph, and then to use each of those four lines as the final lines of four new stanzas. I chose to build my poem from four lines of Page's 'Invisible Presences Fill the Air.' In this poem, the speaker is awestruck to think of presences in the world beyond those that are immediately evident. She works to bring their secret names to light, just as she 'gather[s] their hair for a little suit.' Both comfortably and uncomfortably, she is a collector. This gathering and naming of extra presences of the air reminded me of the American Acclimatization Society's effort, in the 1890s, to ensure that North American skies were populated by every bird mentioned in Shakespeare. This whimsical gesture of introducing species, as living literary allusions, into a natural environment is obviously very consequential. I'm fascinated by the longing this act betrays for a world that is, in some way, designed."

BRENT RAYCROFT was born in Ottawa, has lingered in Montreal and Halifax, and now lives north of Kingston, ON. His poetry has appeared in *Arc, Vallum, Prairie Fire, Freefall, CV2, Queen's Quarterly, The Walrus,* and elsewhere. *The Subtleties of Divine Creatures*, a single poem chapbook, was published in 2014 by Thee Hellbox Press. In 2016, he self-published his mini-epic *Sydenham* to celebrate Canada 175.

Raycroft writes, "Not a 'bad' word itself—in fact much valorized in our day—'sex' nonetheless is the category for the better part of the 'bad' words, and demarcates a special, restricted area. At the same time, we know that sex is supposed to be fun. We sense it bodily, and we're told as much culturally as well. But there are many forces working against the fun: the glamours of porn and advertising, the chill of our anxieties and precautions, the threat, near or distant, of sexual violence. In 'S and X' I've tried taking this overcharged word apart typographically, treating it phonetically, as a sound, but also ideogrammatically—as an image conveying a scene or narrative. I've tried to make the poem inclusive, too, which meant not relying heavily (though it's in the mix) on the formula 'S = woman, X = man.' I imagine that in every sexual relationship, difference, both physical and psychological, is central, and that much of the fun is in the give-and-take, the dialogue, the drama. 'S and X' is a love sonnet, and I flatter myself that it joins that long tradition, but a stronger influence is a writer whose work my children introduced me to: Shel Silverstein."

SHANE RHODES lives in Ottawa. He is the author of six books of poetry including *Dead White Men* (2017, Coach House Books), *X: poems and anti-poems* (2013, Nightwood Editions), and *Err* (2011, Nightwood Editions). Shane's awards include an Alberta Book Award for poetry, two Lampman-Scott Awards, the National Magazine Gold Award for poetry, the P. K. Page Founder's Award for Poetry and a nomination for the Ottawa Book Award.

Of "You Are Here," Rhodes writes, "After a year or two of working on and reading poems from *X*, and trying to explain the project to a number of audiences ('You are writing poems about settler and First Nations relations? About the treaties?' 'You are writing poems with the treaties?!' 'Canada has treaties?'), I decided to address the issue head-on through an introductory poem. I wanted the poem to chant the reader into a different and maybe unexpected historical and political location, a chant that would also respectfully elucidate the strange and contradictory position of any Canadian artist (especially a white artist) writing about the history and present of colonization and race in Canada. 'You Are Here' is an X dropped on a map you may never have seen before."

ELIZABETH ROSS is from Vancouver Island and now lives in Toronto. She's the author of *Kingdom* (Palimpsest, 2015). Her work has appeared in a number of literary magazines, including *The Malahat Review*, *The Fiddlehead*, *Arc*, and most recently, *PRISM international*. When she's not chasing her kids around, she's working on a new collection of poems and a series of memoirs.

Of "Mastiff," Ross writes, "Milton was a huge dog. An English mastiff, he weighed over two hundred and twenty pounds, and, on his hind legs, could look you straight in the eye. He was intimidating. Not only because of his size, but also because of his ability to intuit feelings. The seizures that led from his heart condition were often triggered by our family's anxiety over his health, which he tuned into. He had a huge heart and required honesty, however painful for us or him, from his people. His seizures forced me to consider his breed's history and the intersections of human and animal; I wrote this poem when it looked like we were going to have to put him down. But the beta blockers or the poem or something worked. The seizures didn't take him: he stopped being able to breathe comfortably, lungs obstructed by tumours growing from his heart."

BETH ROWNTREE lives in Vancouver, and if she had her way she would never stop writing. LENORE ROWNTREE lives in Vancouver. She is the author of *Cluck, a novel* (Thistledown Press) and *Dovetail Joint and other stories* (Quadra Books), and the co-editor of *Hidden Lives: true stories from people who live with mental illness* (Brindle & Glass).

Of "7 lbs. 6 oz.," the Rowntrees write, "Two sisters—the similarities are many, the differences few. This poem explores the subtle things that determine who gets a gentle ride in life and who gets a rough one. Many aspects of the poem are found. Emotions found in Lenore's memory, triggered by poems found in Beth's wastebasket, purse, desk, and dresser."

ARMAND GARNET RUFFO was born in Chapleau, northern Ontario, and currently resides in Kingston, where he teaches at Queen's University. Strongly influenced by his Ojibway heritage, his publications include *Water Lily Woman*, a long poem (Textualis Press, 2017), *Introduction to Indigenous Literary Criticism* (Broadview, 2016), *The Thunderbird Poems* (Harbour, 2015) and *Norval Morrisseau: Man Changing Into Thunderbird* (D&M, 2014), a finalist for the Governor General's Literary Award. He continues to publish in a variety of genres.

Of "The Tap is Dripping Memory," Ruffo writes, "In traditional Anishinaabe (Ojibway) culture it's said that we have two souls or spirits. One that is with us during our waking lives, and one that is with us during our sleeping lives. While working on my collection about the acclaimed Anishinaabe painter Norval Morrisseau, whose sense of spirituality is at the centre of his work, I thought a lot about the connection between our inner and outer lives. Am I dreaming or remembering these things? How does the inner dream world inform and shape the outer experiential world? This poem does not try to answer these or any other questions but rather explores the concept by bringing together disparate events at the spirit level."

JOY RUSSELL was born in Belize and lives in North Vancouver. A poet, playwright and writer, her work includes *Days of Old*, a site-specific PodPlay, and has appeared in numerous journals and anthologies such as *Beyond the Pale: Dramatic Writing from First Nation Writers and Writers of Colour*, *Canadian Literature*, *The Capilano Review*, *Crab Orchard Review* and *Bluesprint: Black*

British Columbian Literature and Orature.

Russell writes, "'On King George's Crowning' is part of a poetry manuscript whose eyes and ears fall on Vancouver, London, and Belize, their bodies of water and connection to Empire."

ROBYN SARAH grew up in Montreal, where she still lives. She is the author of ten poetry collections, most recently *My Shoes Are Killing Me*, winner of the Governor General's Literary Award for Poetry in 2015. She has also published two collections of short stories and a book of essays on poetry. Her poems have been broadcast on The Writer's Almanac and included in *The Norton Anthology of Poetry*, and since 2011 she has been poetry editor for Cormorant Books.

Of "Messenger," Sarah writes, "I'm a regular walker on Mount Royal (that oversized pebble in the middle of Montreal to which the name 'mountain' has clung), and like many Montrealers I tend to go straight from boots into sandals in the spring. The serpentine road to the lookout, shared by walkers and cyclists, is a dirt-and-cinder one; bicycle wheels send the fine gravel flying. My poems tend to speak for themselves, but the title of this one is telling: I'm the sort of person who sees messages in things. The proverbial 'stone in the shoe' calls attention to itself in a way that's hard to ignore, yet we seem to have a curious tolerance for it. In this poem, I started out looking for what the stone might be telling me, but ended in the recognition that my own willingness to accommodate it was telling, too. 'Harry my sole' isn't so far from 'Harrow my soul.'"

BRENDA SCHMIDT lives in Creighton, a mining town on the Canadian Shield in northern Saskatchewan. She is the author of four books of poetry and a book of essays. Both her poetry and nonfiction have been shortlisted for Saskatchewan Book Awards. She is a past winner of the Alfred G. Bailey Prize. She founded the Ore Samples Writers Series and serves on the Sage Hill Writing board of directors. In 2017, she became the seventh Saskatchewan Poet Laureate.

Of "A Citizen Scientist's Life Cycle," Schmidt writes, "The epigraph for this poem comes from one of the interviews I conducted for *Culvert Installations*, a book project wherein I consider the way stories emerge and flow. Basically I go through the words I'm given and respond in some way. In this case, the word 'mean' reminded me of a sonnet I'd written after I'd completed a bird survey a few years before. The survey was one of many citizen science projects I've taken part in over the years, though always with a certain uneasiness. The hat of the naturalist has never fit comfortably. There are a number of culverts along the route and I stop near the same ones year after year to search for certain species. This process of returning and searching and the strict constraints of the surveys frequently lead me to the sonnet form, a place where I can argue and tromp around and not scare anything. Sometimes I flush out something new to me, something I hadn't considered before. Naturally the epigraph brought to mind, too, the cycle of seasons and the seasons of life and soon I found myself writing a sonnet cycle using my mean old sonnet as a way in."

DAVID SEYMOUR was born in Campbellton, NB and lives in Toronto, where he works in the film industry. His first book, *Inter Alia*, was published by Brick Books in 2006. His second book, *For Display Purposes Only*, was published by Coach House Books in 2013. He is currently working on his third book, *Lens Flare*.

Seymour writes, "'Song for the Call of the Richardson's Ground Squirrel...' is the result of notes written about my first encounter with the creatures in the prairies. I found their habits and idiosyncrasies fascinating to watch, and sat for hours observing them. That same evening, I also came upon a nest of short-eared owlets, whose cries for food were eerily similar to the alert call of the squirrels."

BARDIA SINAEE was born in Tehran, Iran and lives in Toronto. His poems have appeared in magazines across Canada, including *Arc*, *Maisonneuve*, *The Malahat Review* and *The Walrus*, and in the chapbook, *Blue Night Express* (Anstruther Press, 2015).

Sinaee writes, "'Escape from Statuary' is a self-help poem of sorts. After reading *The Art of Recklessness*, Dean Young's book about poetry, I took to heart his message that poets should forgive themselves for not being perfect. I looked back at my own work and recognized how anxiety about whether or not I was a capital-P poet was manifesting itself as sarcasm, self-loathing, and a sense of preordained failure. 'Escape from Statuary' is my response to this realization. To write it, I indulged in the zealous proclamations most critics hate, and aimed away from the sober, agnostic poetry that vies for a place in the canon and a statue in the park. Therefore it feels delightfully ironic to see the poem anthologized."

SUE SINCLAIR was raised in Newfoundland and is now based in Fredericton, NB, where she writes, edits, and teaches. She is the author of five collections of poetry, most recently *Heaven's Thieves* (Brick Books). All of her books have been nominated for regional and/or national awards. Sue also recently completed a PhD in philosophy on the subject of beauty and ethics, and in 2013 she served as the inaugural Critic-in-Residence for CWILA.

Of "Cherry Trees," Sinclair writes, "Visiting the cherry blossoms in the springtime is one of the few rituals I insist on. I've been wondering if I'm in danger of using up my quota of poems about flowering trees, but if the Japanese can do it for centuries, surely I'm allowed a decade or two."

KAREN SOLIE's latest poetry collection, *The Road In Is Not the Same Road Out*, was published in Canada and the US in 2015. A volume of selected poems, *The Living Option*, was published in the UK in 2013. Her new work has appeared recently in *The Walrus*, *The Paris Review*, *Harper's*, *The London Review of Books*, and *Granta*. An associate director for the Banff Centre's Writing Studio, she lives in Toronto.

Of "Tractor," Solie writes, "Some years ago, my parents bought a new tractor. It is so big they had to construct a new building to put it in. My relationship to it is complicated. The tractor is loud, it burns a lot of fuel, it's expensive to maintain. Machines like it are also necessary to making a living in prairie dryland farming. The poem's second stanza refers to a process by which American-owned (in this case) oil and gas companies drill for gas, a process fraught with hazards and awful byproducts, and one that fuels the tractor. Companies compensate farmers by way of small surface lease payments for the land disturbed by the drilling and truck traffic, a bit of money that helps some farmers continue to make a go of it. (And, since farmers have no mineral rights, if they were to say no to the companies, the companies would simply drill anyway and not pay them.) The tractor is implicated in all of this. It is also an astounding piece of machinery, a marvel of human ingenuity, and really fun to drive."

CARMINE STARNINO was born in Montreal and lives in Toronto. He has published five volumes of poetry, including *This Way Out* (2009), which was nominated for the Governor General's Award. He has won the Canadian Author's Association Prize for Poetry and the A.M. Klein Prize for Poetry. His other books include *Lazy Bastardism: Reviews and Essays on Canadian Poetry* (2012) and *The New Canon: An Anthology of Canadian Poetry* (2005). His most recent collection is *Leviathan* (2016). He is deputy editor for *The Walrus* magazine.

Starnino writes, "Brain research suggests we can actually become addicted to another person; that when we think of them, we get rewarded with dopamine— the same chemical released by taking cocaine. No one warned me such powerful cravings could by experienced by a father toward his newborn son. 'Courtship' came to me fairly quickly, with little revision. I had been rereading Frank O'Hara and James Schuyler, and admired again the simplicity, urgency, and speed of their line-making. I think their process— unforced, direct—helped me capture the obsessiveness of what I was feeling during those early weeks with Lucca."

RICARDO STERNBERG was born in Rio de Janeiro, Brazil and has lived in Toronto since 1979. He has published poetry in magazines such as *Descant*, *The Walrus*, the *Nation*, *Paris Review*, *Poetry* (Chicago) and *American Poetry Review*. He has published four books of poems: *The Invention of Honey* (1990, republished 1996, 2006) and *Map of Dreams* (1996) both with Signal Editions of Véhicule Press and *Bamboo Church* (2003, republished 2006) and *Some Dance* (2014) with McGill-Queen's University Press. ricardosternberg.com

Sternberg writes, "'Blues' is what survives of a sequence of four or five poems begun years ago and centred around a slightly decadent figure called Lord Tamarind. All the poems, like 'Blues,' are composed of five tercets. Years ago on a trip to Europe I was impressed by hearing Andean musicians playing their flutes in every city I visited. The contrast between those mournful tunes sounding out in a metropolitan hubbub stayed with me."

BRUCE TAYLOR lives in Wakefield, QC. He is a two-time winner of the A.M. Klein Award for Poetry. He has published four books of poetry: *Getting On with the Era* (1987), *Cold Rubber Feet* (1989), *Facts* (1998), and *No End in Strangeness* (2011).

Of "Little Animals," Taylor writes, "I was given a book for my fiftieth birthday, an old copy of Clifford Dobell's lovely biography of Antony van Leeuwenhoek, the seventeenth-century Dutch drapier who discovered microbes. Clifford Dobell was himself a microbiologist, an ambitious scientist working in the field van Leeuwenhoek had created. In his spare time, he taught himself Dutch, and translated the old microscopist's letters into English. His book is an affectionate portrait of one curious man by another, and I found it (curiously) moving. Also, it made me want to see these 'animalcules.'"

SOUVANKHAM THAMMAVONGSA was born in the Nong Khai refugee camp in Thailand in 1978. She was raised and educated in Toronto. She is the author of three poetry books, *Small Arguments* (2003), winner of the ReLit Award, *Found* (2007), and *Light* (2013), winner of the Trillium Book Award for Poetry. She is now writer-in-residence at the University of Ottawa.

Of "Gayatri," Thammavongsa writes, "It used to be expensive to take photographs. You didn't get a chance to see how your photograph would turn out before you had them printed. And you had to have them printed in order to see them. I had this photograph of a ceiling and wondered why I had taken a photo of this ceiling. Then I noticed the piece of the tree and remembered how excited I had been about having a real pine tree that Christmas. My childhood best friend, Gayatri, came over after school to look at this real tree and we thought we should take a photograph of ourselves in front of it, but instead I had aimed it at the ceiling and not at us. I didn't know we weren't in the photograph until it was developed and my parents were upset that they had to pay for this photograph of a ceiling. I have not seen Gayatri for almost twenty years and while this photograph does not have her in it, it made me think of her and of us and I saw her in a way I hadn't seen when we were children. I would not have thought so hard and so much of this photograph had we actually been in it. I thought this photograph of the ceiling captured more accurately and precisely the feeling of our friendship than one that included us. To put it another way, the failure of the photograph and the way in which it failed gave me more than one that turned out right. Once I saw that, I felt I had to write a poem about it."

SHARON THESEN was born in Saskatchewan and grew up in small towns across western Canada. She lived in Vancouver until 2003 and now lives in Lake Country, BC. She is Emeritus Professor of Creative Writing at UBC's Okanagan campus and the author of several books of poetry, the most recent being *The Good Bacteria* (2005) and *Oyama Pink Shale* (2011). *The Receiver*, will be published in 2017 by New Star Books.

Of "My Education as a Poet," Thesen writes, "This poem attempts to answer a question similar to the one posed by the late Robert Kroetsch in *Seed Catalogue*: 'how do you grow a poet?' The growing, or education, of a poet is a mysterious and probably fated process, although I have heard it said in many different ways that 'difficulties' have proven to be one of the prerequisites. It seems to me that some poets are 'see-ers'; others are listeners, the category in which I would place my own orientation to poetry. I'm attracted to the truth of rhythm and the vernacular. I'm more a transcriber than a describer of the world and/or consciousness; when I write, I tune myself to an inner reality that is populated with real things, such as banjos, lighters, beaches, cars, can openers, longings, and joy."

SARAH YI-MEI TSIANG lives in Kingston and works in Mississauga at Sheridan College teaching Creative Writing. She has two books of poetry, *Status Update* (shortlisted for the Pat Lowther), and *Sweet Devilry* (winner of the Gerald Lampert) as well as numerous children's books from board books to YA.

Of "Visit," Tsiang writes, "This poem came from a writing exercise by Susan Musgrave. I love the restriction of writing exercises; each one is like a unique formal poem that forces you to stretch beyond your normal writing technique. This particular exercise was to write a ten-line poem in which every line is a lie. I found this exercise intriguing because all the best lies contain an enormous amount of truth. I wanted to walk the balance between things that are formally true/untrue (e.g. my dead father didn't talk to me), as well as the much hazier emotional truths/untruths which tend to overlap and are sometimes the same thing (e.g. everything is a way of remembering/everything is a way of forgetting)."

PRISCILA UPPAL lives in Toronto and is a poet, fiction writer, memoirist, playwright, professor, and Fellow of the Royal Canadian Society. Publications include poetry, *Sabotage, Ontological Necessities* (Griffin Poetry Prize finalist); novels, *The Divine Economy of Salvation, To Whom It May Concern*; and memoir, *Projection: Encounters with My Runaway Mother* (Hilary Weston Prize and Governor General's Award finalist). She's been translated into Croatian, Dutch, French, Greek, Korean, and Italian. *Time Out London* dubbed her "Canada's coolest poet."

Of "To My Suicidal Husband," Uppal writes, "My friend, an internationally renowned biographer, is writing a history of suicide. Her husband killed himself. We met while performing at the Sri Lankan Galle Literary Festival. I was nervous because I had left my husband alone at home when he was still struggling with a critical depression that began after his job was cut during the economic recession. He had attempted suicide earlier in the year and was still at risk. We talked about how one of the worst side-effects is how the sufferer believes their loved ones would be better off without them. My husband believed this. My friend also talked about how people would assume she had an unhappy marriage. This was far from the case. Her husband, like mine, and apparently like most men (research reveals a strong gender division here), was depressed due to work-related stresses. My husband and I had always shared our worlds fully (physical, emotional, intellectual, creative), but depression barred him from mine and I felt barred from his. I worry about how often suicide is represented in art as a romantic option to the distress of living: the beauty of Ophelia floating down a river on the ripples of verse or Anna Karenina disappearing under the train through lines of luminous prose; and how many poets my husband and I admire—Paul Celan, Sylvia Plath, Anne Sexton, Marina Tsvetaeva–ended their own lives. I wanted my husband to know I would never think of his death as beautiful. Only his life is beautiful. And I want to live it with him."

ZACHARIAH WELLS lives in Halifax. He is the author of the poetry collections *Unsettled, Track & Trace and Sum*, and *Career Limiting Moves*, a selection of critical writings. He is editor of *Jailbreaks: 99 Canadian Sonnets* and *The Essential Kenneth Leslie*, and is poetry editor for Biblioasis. A service attendant for Via Rail, he also serves as Chief Shop Steward in Unifor Local 4005.

Wells writes, "I wrote this poem on an Acadian Lines bus to Fredericton,

NB, somewhere between Halifax and Truro, NS, on November 3, 2010. I wrote it quickly—there's only an hour between the two cities—and have changed very little since. That's about all I can say for sure about the origins of 'One and One.' I don't know where it came from—besides the rather obvious, if deceptively complicated, answer 'my mind'—and I am by no means sure what it signifies, though it may well have been influenced in part by my reading of neuroscientist Antonio Damasio's book on self-consciousness *Self Comes to Mind: Constructing the Conscious Brain*. The only edit I made after drafting the poem was the addition of the tag line 'after George Herbert.' This, like so many things in poems, is both true and false. It's true insofar as it was written nearly 400 years after Herbert penned 'Clasping of Hands,' the poem I had in mind when I wrote the tag line. It's false, however, because I hadn't read Herbert's poem prior to composing my own—at least not so far as I can recall, but when you forget as much as I do, anything's possible. Serendipitously, I read 'Clasping of Hands' several weeks after the bus trip that birthed 'One and One,' and I was bowled over by the kinship of syntax and rhetoric in the two poems. I thought it fitting, once they clasped hands in my mind, to wire them 'implacably together.'"

PATRICIA YOUNG was born in Victoria, BC, where she lives today. Her most recent collection of poetry, *Short Takes on the Apocalypse*, was published with Biblioasis. A chapbook of prose poems, *Consider the Paragliders*, is forthcoming with Baseline Press.

Young writes, "Sex between humans is infinitely complex. 'July Baby' is, I suppose, an attempt to look at this complexity in a less than serious manner. Writing it, I was reminded yet again that poetry can be play."

CHANGMING YUAN was born in central China and lives in Vancouver. Growing up in a remote village, he started to learn the English alphabet in Shanghai at age nineteen and published monographs on translation before moving to Canada. With a PhD in English from the University of Saskatchewan, he currently edits *Poetry Pacific* with Allen Qing Yuan; his credits include nine Pushcart nominations, *Best Canadian Poetry* (2009; 2012; 2014), *BestNewPoemsOnline*, *Threepenny Review*, and 1309 others across 39 countries.

JAN ZWICKY grew up in the northwest corner of the Great Central Plain on Treaty 6 territory, was educated at the Universities of Calgary and Toronto, and currently lives on the west coast of Canada. She has published ten collections of poetry, including *Songs for Relinquishing the Earth*, *Forge*, and, most recently, *The Long Walk*. Her books of philosophy include *Lyric*

Philosophy, Wisdom & Metaphor, and *Alkibiades' Love*.

Of "Practising Bach," Zwicky writes, "This poem was commissioned by Tafelmusik Baroque Orchestra and received its first performance in Toronto in January 2007, with Aisslinn Nosky on violin. For each movement, I read the relevant section of the poem, then Aisslinn played. It was a great gift to sense the synergy between the words, Bach's extraordinary music, and Aisslinn's own conception of the piece."

RETROSPECTIVE: OUR GUEST EDITORS' SAMPLER ❧

For our Tenth Anniversary, we offer some prescient and sage highlights from the first nine introductory essays by *Best Canadian Poetry* guest editors.

Stephanie Bolster, 2008
"Introduction"

First: good writing…Second: depth and challenge…Finally an interesting, even strange sensibility or imagination…

As I read 2007's possible contenders—each on several occasions, to increase a poem's chances of striking me in a receptive moment—what was I looking for? First: good writing. Awkward or rote syntax; familiar expressions, images, and locutions; or random lineation, ruled a poem out. A meaningfully rebellious and distinctive syntax or a deliberately dissonant music often ruled it in. Second: depth and challenge, be that emotional or intellectual. If additional readings failed to yield new insights or appreciations, but rather, dulled the flash I'd sensed the first time around, the poem lost its Post-it note. Finally, and inseparably from the first two criteria: an interesting, even strange, sensibility or imagination. (As an undergrad, I fumed when one of my instructors remarked that my poems failed to startle. I didn't want to startle; surely the startle factor was overrated. Only later did I realize that what I did want to do—to please—doomed my poems to mediocrity.) "Startling" need not imply clatter and flash. I sought poems that excited and surprised me, that felt (boldly or quietly) necessary, often urgent.
*

I found very little bad writing. Instead, I read a great deal of competent poetry, most of it in the first-person lyric mode. It was, at times, death (despair, frustration, anger, stupor) by a hundred windows, rivers, aches/hearts/kitchen sinks. I've written about these things, too, and often. I know, from experience, how important it is to find acceptance of one's work, especially early in one's career. I recognize that journals have commitments to subscribers and funding bodies, that prevent editors from simply deciding not to publish in a given season or to whittle an issue down to a flyer's scantiness.
*

While every poem that is written deserves to have been written, every poem that is published does not merit publication.

A.F. Moritz, 2009
"Canadian Poetry Today"

The poems here defend faith and hope in human life and in the earth. They uphold the sense, primordial within us, that earthly life for all its hardships and problems is a good gift, the hope that human existence is not pointless...

When we feel the impulse of expression, this is the world, our world, coming to birth in a new form. We might recall what John Donne has told us about worlds: each of us "has one and is one." From this recognition springs the freshness that sweeps through the mind upon reading a simple poem, or all at once understanding something of a difficult one, in getting the idea for one, or working on it over hours, months, years, or at last finishing it properly. Our world has flowered. Its former brightness, without ceasing to be bright, is revealed to have been a rich darkness from which the world has now burst into further light.

*

The poems here defend faith and hope in human life and in the earth. They uphold the sense, primordial within us, that earthly life for all its hardships and problems is a good gift, the hope that human existence is not pointless, is not reducible to doings and distractions that for each of us end up six feet under. But on the other hand, our contemporary poetry most certainly does not preach, does not take up a message. On the contrary. What has happened is that the modern threats to hope, and to life itself, have simply revealed to poetry certain dimensions of its primordial and constant nature. In a situation such as ours today, these dimensions naturally tend to come to the fore, without poetry having to sacrifice any of its spontaneity, anarchy, and imaginative independence. It protests, and evinces a truer way, simply by being what it is in and against the often thin, hateful cultural context it finds around it.

*

A thought of mine, for which Avison would be a classic illustration, is that the greatest intensity lies in the most perfect balance of forces, which looks to the observer like a sort of repose, often referred to as harmony. And it is indeed a true "repose," a re-placing and repositioning of our reality on a new footing. But it is tense with all power. It is the very opposite of the mere non-activity resulting from the absence of motivation or impinging forces. And it is also the very opposite of what is usually taken for intensity: a going to the extreme in one direction or another, which is in fact only a minor and distorted intensity, the development or release of one tendency while the others remain infantile.

The power of such balance, or the drama of the quest for it, or the longing or the suffering in its absence: these are the essential contents of good poetry.

Lorna Crozier, 2010
"Holding Feathers in Your Teeth"

Poetry takes us back to the sensory quality of the words themselves, their syllabics and accents, their sibilance, clicks, guffaws, moans.

Word by word a poem is built. The choice of one over another implies an attitude and reflects the writer's beliefs, insights, and character. Think of forestry bosses calling the killing of trees "harvesting," or of Dick Cheney calling water boarding "robust interrogation." Albert Camus went so far as to say, "Naming an object inaccurately means adding to the unhappiness of the world."
*

It is this scrupulous, engaging attention to diction, along with the sad acknowledgement that words can't be collared and brought to heel, that sets poetry apart from other genres and one poem apart from another. In a good poem the words are charged with a potency and precision that would be envied by the most punctilious scientist.
*

And then, there's metaphor. Aristotle claimed that metaphor-making is a skill that can't be taught. Metaphoric language, which includes the simile and metonymy, is a sacred trope. Its bringing together of two unlike objects creates a newborn thing, not an invention but a discovery of something primal, something we have missed, as if the writer has pulled the string of a light bulb in an earth-walled cellar. A metaphor that is both apt and transcendent, that feels both ancient and novel, reminds us that all things are connected, even man and animal, dark and light, breath and non-breath. Metaphor spells out what Beaudelaire called "the universal correlation."
*

The language of poetry does more than mean and more than solder one thing to another to make an exquisite, new-fangled fit that holds. Poetry takes us back to the sensory quality of the words themselves, their syllabics and accents, their sibilance, clicks, guffaws, moans.
*

The ecological poems in this anthology, though they confront in sad and vital imagery the sorrows our species has brought to the world, make me feel hope. It is a hope that has something to do with the enraptured concentration the poets have brought to their subjects and their joyous and evident delight in putting to use our soiled and cadenced Canadian English. The varied metaphors, images, music, and forms of these poems enact our planet's glorious though disappearing diversity, illuminated by the fire of poetic attention.

Priscila Uppal, 2011
"Connected Dots"

I read whenever and wherever I could: over tea in the morning, on the subway, on trains and airplanes, in doctor's offices, in university common areas between classes, restaurants, in the CBC lobby, on Bajan beaches, during intermissions at the opera, intermissions at hockey games, in hotel rooms, in bed, beside pools, in parks, before readings, even on long elevator rides.

For those interested in the editorial process, I dedicated four boxes and two folders in my office to this project. Boxes: 1) To Read; 2) Read (poems of interest noted); 3) Read (no poems of interest); 4) Not Eligible… Folders: 1) Poems to be Considered (photocopied, all bibliographic info listed); 2) List of Magazines and Journals submitted. I read whenever and wherever I could: over tea in the morning, on the subway, on trains and airplanes, in doctor's offices, in university common areas between classes, restaurants, in the CBC lobby, on Bajan beaches, during intermissions at the opera, intermissions at hockey games, in hotel rooms, in bed, beside pools, in parks, before readings, even on long elevator rides.
*

Let me admit that I couldn't get a certain song out of my head: "TV II" by industrial metal band Ministry, now retired but popular with angry disgruntled youth like me in the 90s. It's a song whose lyrics I used to scream at the top of my lungs whenever I really needed to let off steam, and it replays in my head whenever I'm stuck reading what I deem to be predictable poem after sentimental poem after banal poem after derivative poem after lazy poem after unmemorable poem…

Tell me something I don't know
Show me something I can't use
Push the button
Connect the goddamn dots

I could quote aesthetic principles and poetics theories from a wide range of poetic manifestoes from Canada, the US, Europe, and elsewhere (which would admittedly make for a very interesting discussion, but one too lengthy for these pages), but I can also tell you with confidence that the above four lines reflect quite accurately my aesthetic and theoretical criteria for poem selection.

*

Sure, as any Canadian literature professor will tell you, we write landscape poems, and love poems, and elegies, and odes, and family poems, and historical poems, fixed form poems, and identity poems (geographic and ethnic and cultural), but lots of poets are writing them in exciting, unconventional ways. We write poems that challenge the definitions of the "literary" poetic canons or centres; we are home to an accomplished visual poetry, conceptual poetry, spoken word and sound poetry scene. We write found poems, prose poems, academic poems, and collaborative works. We are meditative and intellectual, brash and angry, elegant and graceful, nostalgic and reverent, unsentimental and irreverent, serious and politically engaged, locally focused and globally aware. And we're also funny. Funny, and clever, and playful, and ironic.

*

I've been informed that there are always a lot of bear poems, gun poems, drinking poems, dog-walking poems, poems about poetry, landscape poems, Adam and Eve poems, and fruit poems; this year was no different...

Carmine Starnino, 2012
"Steam Punk Zone"

But something else defines this group. They are the first generation for whom the battle lines of mainstream versus avant-garde ...have outlived their usefulness.

Heeding this carnival voice has turned the recent scene into a teeming bazaar, where younger poets proudly wear the bright, patchwork clothes of their cosmopolitan nurturing. But something else defines this group. They are the first generation for whom the battle lines of mainstream versus avant-garde (what an earlier time dubbed "cooked" and "raw") have outlived their usefulness. The intense need to set free a shifting sense of self has helped produce the unusual range of devices in this book: intricate puns, up-to-the-minute slang, scat-singing wordplay, many-sided metaphors. These devices are brandished by poets who have not only come out on the other side of the poetry wars, but aspire to heal the divisions.

*

If Canadian poetry were a sci-fi novel, it would take place in 1900 London with robots, goggle-donning hackers, airships, gear-driven computers and zombie hordes.

*

There's a difference between a game and a poem. Both should be played with as much skill as possible, but a game is played for its own sake, while a poem, and our pleasure in its gambits, depends on the recognition it is saying something true about life. A poem, essentially, is a game with a single price of admission: that its rules aren't cut off from the sadness, exultation or distress that pushed the poet to fashion those rules in the first place.

*

...to rebuild the foundations of the lyric from scratch, to submit their nonpareil concoctions as counterprogramming for the Canadian canon. And yet that strikes me as the easy part; made obvious by the scores of poets doing it. Such poetry is frequently over-deliberate; a didactic version of originality, one that keeps insisting on its novelty. Much of it testifies, at best, to the presence of a creative habit, but not the intensity of art.

*

Canadian poets generate, as if on automatic, wonderful contrivances from disparate materials. These are poets who care about their poetry and work hard at it. Like watchmakers, they build machines out of the minutest parts; unlike watches, these machines are full of beguiling generosity for errant incidents. But too often we are faced with an artificial intelligence, simulated for believability, not an actual style. Style is what happens when originality becomes indistinguishable from the poem itself. It's a way of mingling the unfamiliar "new" and the still-compelling "old" so that we can no longer separate them. Style is therefore what happens when a voice is so grounded in its subject the effect is not a self-regarding newness but a newness absorbed into the poem, a newness ripening into something effortlessly manifold and available. Such poems may not be the sort fusionists like, but they are the sort real poets write.

Sue Goyette, 2013
"Inviting the guests..."

Good art is hospitable...

And I like the idea that good art is hospitable, that it's aerated with the kind of silence that invites participation, a private leaning in. I'm thinking of the

Dutch artist, Theo Jansen. His Strandbeests are contraptions made of plastic tubing that lie flat on the beach and, with the right wind, rise and move. Like a poem. Left on the page and when encountered by its reader, rises and briefly moves with that reader's breath.

*

And art, Jeanette Winterson told us, objects. It objects to the rush, the schedule, the malls, the headlines of these times. It defies the idea of commodity and insists on being what it is: in this case, poems. Not a break or a distraction from our times but rather a way for us to recharge in order to better face them. A shelter with some rope and chocolate, a bottle of wine, matches left for the lost mountain climbers who happen to find it. Art as a kind of pay it forward for each other.

*

I chose these poems because I like them. They've got a vitality that instigates more vitality. There's a presence to them à la Marina Abramovic. They maintain eye contact, they attend and abide. They're actualized, and by that I mean they've been allowed to be the shape, the rhythm, the size they need to be. Whoever was at their helm knew how to get out of their way. Their poets kept distraction at bay and stayed true to the work of making something original, imaginative, unexpected and with the voltage that a realized contraption has that is part delight, part surprise and part spur to our appetite for more. For more poems that leave us startled by how simple, how easy a good poem moves. Like water over rocks. How words, treated in this atmosphere, become bigger than themselves. Verdant. How we didn't realize how much we needed words like this in this order. How they call our best self forth to do something. Anything.

Sonnet L'Abbé, 2014
"'Best' isn't a Beauty Contest: How Canadian Poets Demand More of Verse"

...a point of light in darkness, with the power to illuminate its surroundings and to draw and focus a wandering attention... poetry spurs out amongst disease, mercenary practices, racism.

(The quoted passages in the highlights below are from Sharon Thesen's "My Education as a Poet," a poem Sonnet selected for her edition and subsequently used as a framework for her discussion of poetics.)

The kind of curation I want to practice, here and elsewhere, is less about holding new work up against a set of performance indicators and measuring, and more about being able to recognize and celebrate the way new work takes up values indicated by the genre's conventions. Genre is the frame that allows us to talk about writing without simply saying, "It's all poetry! Ergo it's all wonderful!"... Calling a work a poem, then, guarantees nothing about its form, suggests little about any rules of execution it might follow, but rather invites us to appreciate the writing for doing, or consciously challenging, things that poetry has traditionally done well.

*

Thesen's autobiographical, narrative poem ultimately asserts that any life, any growing-up in any place, is full of moments of poetry. Her education has been to learn to recognize them.

*

A simple "*hushabye, lullabye,*" is one of the first such moments in Thesen's poem, suggesting that the early pleasures of repetition and cadence, of the musicality of language, form the foundational awareness of the poet.

*

"Poetry: a bright flame." In this definition, I see poetry figured as a point of light in darkness, with the power to illuminate its surroundings and to draw and focus a wandering attention.

*

One of my favourite Thesen-isms: "*Poetry: a can opener.*" On one level, sure, poetry often opens up a sustaining can of soul food for a hungry spiritual traveller, or opens up a can of worms, speaking of things that other public discourse will not. But I also saw in Thesen's image a "real" red-handled can opener, sitting on a white plinth, as Duchamp's urinal once hung on a white gallery wall, with a little tag beside the opener that reads, "Poetry." A Dadaist interpretation of Thesen's definition allows poetry to be almost anything that one wants to call poetry, and makes room for the broadest interpretation of defamiliarization, of "making strange," as one of the values we can bring to our appreciation of poetry.

*

Poetry: off on an angle. Thesen's idea of poetry intersects, or even has its origin in, a human reality that is decidedly not its rarefied spaces; that is, not necessarily from its libraries, chapels or contemplative gardens; poetry spurs out amongst disease, mercenary practices, racism. I read Thesen as insisting on poetry's place as a response to life's challenges and excesses, as a path by which we redirect energies such as sorrow, resistance, desire, and even fleeting joy into order and beauty. If there is one thing that all the poems in this anthology have in common, it is that they affirm the simple and fundamental value of being-in-the-world, of being in all its nameable and unnameable forms.

Jacob McArthur Mooney, 2015
"The South-facing Window"

An accessible poem is just an advertisement for a poem, while a good difficult one is a proof, a demonstration of the wildness available within the domesticated urges of our language.

The Best Canadian Poetry in English series stands at the same frontier as the window. It is made by those on our side as a kind of yearbook, summarizing and specifying changes in our culture, holding new voices up against the established. But, unlike a yearbook, it plugs into a broader access and is read by those on the other side of the window, too, those whose interest in poetry is more transient. For people who spend great amounts of their time, as I do, trying to coax people through the door and into the poetry-centric side of the glass, the lead concerns I bring to the task of guest editing this year's version are: What is welcoming, exactly? What opens the door and keeps it open?

I am happy to report that there are no Accessible Poems in this anthology... What I have done is try to include poems that are difficult, but in a variety of ways. Difficult, in the end, is reader-loving. Accessible, in the end, is a restraint. I have a great deal of faith in anyone who has crossed the great ocean of legal entertainments and picked this specific book out of the crowd, and I want to repay that unusual trust. An accessible poem is just an advertisement for a poem, while a good difficult one is a proof, a demonstration of the wildness available within the domesticated urges of our language.

If we say that the product of a great poem is the adoption of disparate or even opposite simultaneous reactions in the head of a reader, if you come to experience joy and shame or umbrage and optimism all at once, if you come to understand the window as both fronting and not fronting on the lake, then this may be the most difficult and transcendent game poetry can play...

...for my dollar, most of the great work is being done in a post-Canadian moment. By post-Canadian, I want to dismiss not national themes but rather national mechanics, an idea of poetry and place that treats the nation, its environment and people, as some kind of perfectible vessel made whole by myth and wisdom.

Another good border zone is the Canadian Poetry section of our country's chain bookstores...The big box stores have the arbitrariness of scale; they aren't assembled lovingly by a knowing hand and are instead the product of shipping patterns and stock overruns. In their own blunt way, they are a public... Maybe you are reading these words right now in the Canadian poetry grotto of a Chapters or Coles, considering where to spend your Art Dollar. I wonder how many of these poems you, individual reader, will like. What's a good number? Surely if you read through the book and say "All fifty" I'll know you're either lying or I've failed to make an adequately varied, adequately conflicted contribution as a guest editor. But if you read them and say "None," I won't believe you either.

Helen Humphreys, 2016
"Wild at Heart"

Good writing is a delicate balance of receptivity and control.

It is not form, or lack of form, or intellectual fervor, or exquisite lyricism that makes a good poem in my world, but rather it is a poem that has a little piece of wilderness at its heart. What I mean by "wilderness" is that there is a quality or aspect to the poem that exists because of the poem itself, not because it was orchestrated or carefully inserted there by the poet. This "wilderness" is something that has taken the poet by surprise and therefore also takes the reader by surprise, and it is this small turn, this surprise, that makes both poet and reader forget themselves and fully enter the world of the poem.
*
Good writing is a delicate balance of receptivity and control. Receptivity is a willingness to explore and experiment, to be vulnerable to life and all its teachings... The best writing exposes the vulnerabilities of the writer, doesn't keep them hidden, and in the way that much of life is paradoxical, the vulnerability becomes the strength of the work.

INDEX TO POEMS ♋

Within each subject, the last names of authors of relevant poems are listed alphabetically. Poems in this anthology are printed alphabetically by author's last name.

Neilson, Shane (father & daughter)
Nguyen, Hoa (mother & daughter)
Partridge, Elise (father & son)
Rowntree, Lenore & Beth (sisters)
Ruffo, Armand Garnet (family &
  community)
Starnino, Carmine (father & son)
Thesen, Sharon (father, mother &
  daughter)
Tsiang, Sarah Yi-Mei (father &
  daughter)

Farm
Margoshes, David
Neilson, Shane
Solie, Karen

Friends
Fernandes, Raoul
Ladouceur, Ben
McCarney, Sadie
Pierson, Ruth Roach
Thammavongsa, S.

History & geopolitics
Babstock, Ken
Barger, John Wall
Barton, John
Bowling, Time
Clarke, George Elliott
Good, Michelle
Graham, Laurie D
Howard, Sean
Khâsha
Lambert, Sandra
Lebowitz, Rachel
Lee, Dennis
McCarney, Sadie
Mooney, Jacob McArthur
Morgan, Cara-Lyn
Nguyen, Hoa
Rhodes, Shane
Ruffo, Armand Garnet
Russell, Joy
Seymour, David

Taylor, Bruce
Thesen, Sharon

Horticulture
Avison, Margaret
Bolster, Stephanie
Dalton, Mary
L'Abbé, Sonnet
Leedahl, Shelley A.
Margoshes, David
Sinclair, Sue
Young, Patricia

Identity
Avison, Margaret
Bowling, Time
Coles, Don
Crawford, Lucas
Dempster, Barry
Meijer, Sadiqa de
Graham, Laurie D
Heighton, Steven
Humpheys, Helen
Jernigan, Amanda
Khâsha
Lau, Evelyn
Margoshes, David
Mooney, Jacob McArthur
Morgan, Cara-Lyn
Neilson, Shane
Nguyen, Hoa
Page, P.K.
Pierson, Ruth Roach
Ruffo, Armand Garnet
Russell, Joy
Sarah, Robyn
Sternberg, Ricardo
Sinaee, Bardia
Thesen, Sharon
Yuan, Changming

MAGAZINES CONSULTED FOR BEST CANADIAN POETRY ⟨𝔰

The Antigonish Review. PO Box 5000, Antigonish, NS B2G 2W5. antigonishreview.com

Arc Poetry Magazine. PO Box 81060, Ottawa, ON K1P 1B1. arcpoetry.ca

Ascent Aspirations (defunct)

B after C. 260 Ryding Avenue, Toronto, ON M6N 1H5.

Branch Magazine (defunct)

Brick. PO Box 609, Stn. P, Toronto, ON M5S 2Y4. brickmag.com

Bywords. bywords.ca

Canadian Broadcasting Corporation, CBC Poetry Prize finalists. cbc.ca

Canadian Literature. University of British Columbia, 8-6303 N.W. Marine Dr., Vancouver, BC V6T 1Z1. canlit.ca

Canadian Notes & Queries. 1520 Wyandotte St. East, Windsor, ON, N9A 3L2. notesandqueries.ca

Canadian Poetries (defunct)

The Capilano Review. 102-281 Industrial Ave., Vancouver, BC V6A 2P2. thecapilanoreview.ca

Carousel. UC 274, University of Guelph, Guelph, ON N1G 2W1. carouselmagazine.ca

C magazine. PO Box 5 Stn B, Toronto Ontario, M5T 2T2. Cmagazine.com

Contemporary Verse 2 (CV2). 502-100 Arthur St., Winnipeg, MB R3B 1H3. contemporaryverse2.ca

Dalhousie Review. Dalhousie University, Halifax, NS B3H 4R2. dalhousiereview.dal.ca

Descant (defunct)

ditch. ditchpoetry.com (defunct)

enRoute Magazine. Spafax Canada, 4200 Boul. Saint-Laurent, Ste. 707, Montréal, QC H2W 2R2. enroute.aircanada.com

Event. PO Box 2503, New Westminster, BC V3L 5B2. www.eventmagazine.ca

Exile Quarterly. Exile/Excelsior Publishing Inc., 170 Wellington Street West, PO Box 308, Mount Forest, ON, N0G 2L0. theexilewriters.com

Existere. Vanier College 101E, York University, 4700 Keele St. Toronto, ON M3J 1P3. yorku.ca/existere

The Fiddlehead. Campus House, University of New Brunswick, 11 Garland Ct., PO Box 4400, Fredericton, NB E3B 5A3. thefiddlehead.ca

filling Station. PO Box 22135, Bankers Hall, Calgary, AB T2P 4J5. fillingstation.ca

Forget Magazine. 810-1111, Melville St., Vancouver, B.C. V6E 3V6. forgetmagazine.com

Freefall Magazine. 460, 1720, 29th Street West, Calgary AB, T2T 6T7. freefallmagazine.ca

Geist. Suite 210, 111 W. Hastings St., Vancouver, BC V6B 1H4. geist.com

Grain. PO Box 3986, Regina, SK, S4P 3R9. grainmagazine.ca

Hazlitt. penguinrandomhouse.ca/hazlitt

The Humber Literary Review. humerliteraryreview.com

The Impressment Gang. theimpressmentgang.com

The Leaf. PO Box 2259, Port Elgin, ON N0H 2C0. brucedalepress.ca

Lemon Hound. lemonhound.com

The Literary Review of Canada. 706-170 Bloor St. W., Toronto, ON M5S 1T9. reviewcanada.ca

Maisonneuve. 1051 boul. Decarie, PO Box 53527, Saint Laurent, QC H4L 5J9 maisonneuve.org.

The Malahat Review. University of Victoria, PO Box 1700, Stn. CSC, Victoria, BC V8W 2Y2. malahatreview.ca

Maple Tree Literary Supplement. 1103-1701 Kilborn Ave., Ottawa, ON K1H 6M8. mtls.ca

Matrix. 1455 Blvd. de Maisonneuve, Montreal, QC H3G 1M8. matrixmagazine.org

New Poetry. newpoetry.ca

The New Quarterly. St. Jerome's University, 290 Westmount Rd. N, Waterloo, ON N2L 3G3. tnq.ca

Numéro Cinq. numerocinqmagazine.com

One Throne. onethrone.com

ottawater. ottawater.com

Our Times. 407-15 Gervais Dr., Toronto, ON M3C 1Y8. ourtimes.ca

(parenthetical). wordsonpagespress.com/parenthetical

Partisan partisanmagazine.com

Poetry Is Dead. 5020 Frances St., Burnaby, BC V5B 1T3. www.poetryisdead.ca

Prairie Fire. 423-100 Arthur St., Winnipeg, MB R3B 1H3. prairiefire.ca

PRISM International. Creative Writing Program, University of British Columbia, Buchanan Room E462, 1866 Main Mall, Vancouver, BC V6T 1Z1. prismmagazine.ca

Pulp Literature. pulpliterature.com

The Puritan. puritan-magazine.com

Queen's Quarterly. Queen's University, 144 Barrie St., Kingston, ON K7L 3N6. queensu.ca/quarterly

Rampike (defunct)

Ricepaper. PO Box 74174, Hillcrest RPO, Vancouver, BC V5V 5L8. ricepapermagazine.ca

Room. PO Box 46160, Stn. D, Vancouver, BC V6J 5G5. roommagazine.com

The Rotary Dial. therotarydial.ca

The Rusty Toque. therustytoque.com

17 Seconds. ottawater.com/seventeenseconds

The Steel Chisel. thesteelchisel.ca

subTerrain. PO Box 3008, MPO, Vancouver, BC V6B 3X5. subterrain.ca

Taddle Creek. PO Box 611, Stn. P, Toronto, ON M5S 2Y4. taddlecreekmag.com

This Magazine. 417-401 Richmond St. W, Toronto, ON M5V 3A8. this.org

Toronto Quarterly. (defunct)

Vallum. 5038 Sherbrooke W., PO BOX23077, CP Vendome, Montreal, QC H4A 1T0. vallummag.com

The Walrus. 411 Richmond St. E., Suite B15, Toronto, ON, M5A 3S5 walrusmagazine.com

West Coast Line. (defunct)

Windsor Review. Department of English, University of Windsor, 401 Sunset Ave., Windsor, ON N9B 3P4. windsorreview.wordpress.com

Untethered. alwaysuntethered.com

Zouch Magazine. zouchmagazine.com

Details and rules for Best Canadian Poetry Series

Each year, the fifty best poems and the list of notable poems are selected from more than sixty print and online journals, as listed above. No poems may be submitted directly to the anthology. All poems chosen must be published in the previous year in a Canadian print or online periodical. We depend on those periodicals to keep us updated on their issues. If you edit or publish a print or online journal that does not appear on our list of magazines consulted, please inform us of your url at bookinfo@tightropebooks.com, or add Best Canadian Poetry, c/o Tightrope Books (#207-2 College St., Toronto, ON, M5G 1K3) to your roster of complementary subscribers.

This year's special anniversary edition comprises a selection of poems chosen by the series editors from all previous editions of *The Best Canadian Poetry in English*.

PERMISSION ACKNOWLEDGEMENTS ☙

"Autumn News From the Donkey Sanctuary" from *Methodist Hatchet* copyright © 2011 by Ken Babstock. Reprinted with permission from House of Anansi Press, Toronto, www.anansi.ca.

"Urgent Message from the Captain of the Unicorn Hunters" copyright © 2014 by John Wall Barger. Reprinted with permission of the author.

"Turing's Machine" was originally published in *Polari* copyright © 2014 by John Barton. Reprinted with permission of Goose Lane Editions.

"Flight" copyright © 2008 by Shirley Bear. Reprinted with permission of the author.

"The Roll Call to the Ark" from *As If A Raven* copyright © 2014 by Yvonne Blomer. Reprinted with permission of Palimpsest Press.

"Gardening" copyright © 2011 by Stephanie Bolster. Reprinted with permission of the author.

"Union Local 64" from *Circa Nineteen Hundred and Grief* copyright © 2014 by Tim Bowling. Reprinted with permission of Gaspereau Press.

"Dante's Ikea" from *Skullduggery* copyright © 2011 by Asa Boxer. Reprinted with permission of Signal Editions.

"Two Fish" copyright © 2014 by Julie Bruck. Reprinted with permission of the author.

"Father's Old Blue Cardigan" copyright © 2012 by Anne Carson. Reprinted with permission of the author.

"Notes from the Canary Islands" copyright © 2010 by Peter Chiykowski. Reprinted with permission of the author.

"A Letter from Henry Tucker, August 28, 1789" copyright © 2013 by George Elliott Clarke. Reprinted with permission of the author.

"Memory, Camus, Beaches" copyright © 2010 by Don Coles. Reprinted with permission of the author.

"Stars, Sunday Dawn" from *Asking Questions Indoors and Out* (Fitzhenry & Whiteside, 2009) copyright © 2009 by Anne Compton. Reprinted with permission.

"Salvage" copyright © 2011 by Dani Couture. Reprinted with permission of the author.

Tightrope Books gratefully acknowledges the authors and publishers for permission to reprint the copyrighted works in this book. Every effort has been made to obtain permission for the use of copyrighted material. The publisher apologizes for any errors or omissions in the above list and would be grateful if notified of any corrections so that acknowledgement may be made in subsequent editions.

EDITOR BIOGRAPHIES ☙

ANITA LAHEY is a poet, journalist, reviewer, and essayist. She is the author of *The Mystery Shopping Cart: Essays on Poetry and Culture* (Palimpsest Press, 2013) and of two Véhicule Press poetry collections: *Out to Dry in Cape Breton* (2006) and *Spinning Side Kick* (2011). The former was shortlisted for the Trillium Book Award for Poetry and the Ottawa Book Award. Anita is a former editor of *Arc Poetry Magazine*, and posts occasionally on her blog, "Henrietta & Me: People and other wonders found in books."

MOLLY PEACOCK is a widely anthologized poet and writer. Her seventh volume of poetry is *The Analyst*, poems about psychoanalysis, poetry, and painting, from Biblioasis. Her recent book of tiny tales is *Alphabetique: 26 Characteristic Fictions*, with illustrations by Kara Kosaka; she is also the author of a biography, *The Paper Garden: Mrs. Delany Begins Her Life's Work at 72*, and a memoir, *Paradise, Piece by Piece*, all from McClelland & Stewart.